TRAVAILS OF NOVICE PRINCIPALS AS FISCAL MANAGERS

A Thesis Proposal Presented to
The Faculty of the Professional School
University of Mindanao, Davao City

In Partial Fulfillment of the Requirements for the Degree of
Master of Arts in Education, Major in Educational Management

JULIE ANN D. BAYANI
&
EUNICE A. ATIENZAR, EDD

December 2022

ISBN: 978-1-957114-57-6 (Paperback)
ISBN: 978-1-957114-58-3 (eBook)

i

APPROVAL SHEET

This thesis entitled **"TRAVAILS OF NOVICE PRINCIPALS AS FISCAL MANAGERS"** prepared and submitted by JULIE ANN D. BAYANI in partial fulfillment of the requirements for the degree of MASTER OF ARTS IN EDUCATION major in Educational Management, has been examined and is thereby recommended for thesis proposal and outline defense.

EUNICE A. ATIENZAR, EdD

Adviser

PANEL OF EXAMINERS

APPROVED by the Panel of Examiners an Oral Examination with a grade of _____.

EUGENIO S. GUHAO, JR., D.M.

Chairman

Member: **JOEL B. TAN, CPA/DBA**   Member: **JOCELYN B. BACASMOT, PhD**

Member: **EDWIN NEBRIA, PhD**   Member: **RINATE L. GENUBA, EdD**

ACCEPTED in partial fulfillment of the requirement for the degree,

MASTER OF EDUCATION major in Educational Management.

Comprehensive Examination : _____

ACKNOWLEDGEMENT

I would like to express my heartfelt thanks to God Almighty, the source of all wisdom and knowledge, for making it possible for me to overcome all obstacles in completing this study.

I'd also like to thank the following people:

Dr. Eunice Atienzar, my adviser, for her unwavering leadership, unending support, and invaluable thoughtfulness;

The panel members: Dr. Joel B. Tan, Jocelyn Bacasmot, Rinante L. Genuba, and Edwin Nebria, for their comments, constructive criticism, corrections, and ideas to enhance the study;

Dr. Reynaldo M. Guillena, CESO V, Davao City Division Schools Division Superintendent, for letting me perform the study.

Special acknowledgment to my Transform Global Faith Ministry family, who have been my prayer partners and constantly remind me that I am called for such a purpose that God has in store for me.

DEDICATION

I dedicate this work to my Savior, Lord Jesus, for always lighting the way for me in this learning journey. Your still, small voice whispered to me to push through and never give up on every doubt and worry that crossed my mind. As a result of my efforts in this lifetime's calling, this accomplishment belongs to You.

I also dedicate this paper to my family, starting with my papa, who has always been my encourager. My mother, who may not have been with me over the years, she's still been one of the reasons I have achieved great things in life. And, of course, to my three brothers, who always stand by me whenever I need them.

I also want to dedicate this study to my current Communal National High School. All the people there, especially my students, become one of the motivations for why I strive to be a better person and an excellent educator.

I would remember to dedicate this research to the future school leaders who aspire to bring positive changes; keep pushing through!

ABSTRACT

This phenomenological study aimed to set guidelines for future school leaders as fiscal managers. The study utilized a qualitative research design with a phenomenological approach with six new principals that were chosen through purposive homogeneous sampling, which used thematic analysis as a data analysis tool by utilizing an interview guide. The findings revealed that school leaders experienced the following during their early years: a constant need to plan for school improvement; difficulty addressing school concerns, particularly those concerning school resources; uncertainty about the factors to consider when handling school finances; and a range of emotions as a school leader. In coping mechanisms, they find these things important such as collaboration with mentors and colleagues; continuous learning and updating; ingenuity and resourcefulness; and being open and optimistic. Moreover, the participants mentioned their learning insights: act in our role as the school head; connect with our mentors and peers in the field; be literate in fiscal management; and be receptive and willing to learn. Indeed, schools need leaders to handle finances as they affect the organization, so this study sets guidelines to help future school principals as fiscal managers.

Keywords: travails; novice principals; fiscal management; phenomenological; NVIVO software; thematic analysis; Philippines

TABLE OF CONTENTS

CHAPTER 5 DISCUSSION

Chapter 1

INTRODUCTION

Rationale

This study focuses on new school principals' difficulties during their first to third year on the job, particularly in managing school finances. As it says, a leadership role is challenging (Kuligowski, 2022), given that there are many challenges you have to go through when you are in the position. Most school principals find the job difficult since they need help with many things, like administrative tasks and financial management. This includes dealing with disgruntled or unhappy teachers and other employees who may try to undermine the principal's authority, which drains their energy (Harper, 2018).

Moreover, while school heads are perceived to be skilled, competent, and compassionate, these qualities cannot compensate for basic school needs, which is why the organization requires a school leader who is experienced in financial management, as it has a significant impact on the quality of education along the way.

Fiscal management among novice school heads is critical in decision-making, as they are responsible for not only protecting, developing, and using resources, pushing and maintaining economic growth, and increasing income but also effectively and efficiently managing all school resources (Arrieta & Ancho, 2020). If finances are mismanaged, it can significantly affect the school's overall performance. Mismanagement is a significant failure to carry out the responsibility to lead and manage an institution or an administration (Spacey, 2020). Thus, financial mismanagement is management that is done in a way that can be described as "wrong, bad, negligent, inefficient, or inept" and has a detrimental impact on a company's or individual's financial condition. Financial mismanagement can be carried out in a variety of ways. For example, proper responsibility distribution, consistency with payments, bills, and taxes disregarding responsibilities, financial difficulties, and economic status can result in significant financial mismanagement (Nathaniel, 2019).

Furthermore, this paper is anchored first in the study of Butt (2010), which suggests that efficient use and adherence to financial management practices lead to increased business performance. Companies that are well-managed financially are also operationally efficient. This is a positive sign for investors and regulatory bodies. These might also help organizations get a competitive advantage in future forecasting. The second proposition is about learning by doing. According to David Kolb, this type of learning is the process by which information is formed via the transformation of experience, knowledge coming from the combination of comprehending and modifying experience (Cherry, 2020).

Adding on, because school principals shoulder enormous responsibilities, many need help grasping the scope of their duties and reliability in accounting and finance (Shkurina, 2018). Accounting and financial reporting are the cruces of a school's economic and academic success. On this note, the researcher was motivated to embark on this study to find out and understand the lived experiences and struggles of novice principals as fiscal managers. Moreover, after reviewing various literature, it was discovered that there was no similar study, especially in local and global settings. Thus this study will contribute to the avoidance of unnecessary mistakes, such as what happened in an Illinois private school, which ran a one-million-plus deficit in 2014 due to a wrong account being accidentally used. As a result, the school got buried in debt worth hundreds of thousands of dollars for years to come. (Shkurina, 2018).

Purpose of the Study

This qualitative study aims to guide future school leaders, particularly in financial management. As we all know, being a first-timer or newbie is not simple, so the insights gained here will be beneficial to us, not only as a researcher but also as hopeful individual who hopes to become school leader one day if God permits. This study focuses on the real-life experiences of new principals who have already served for 1–3 years.

This research allows us to broaden our social experiences with this group of school principals. We could connect with their opinions, beliefs, and feelings during the interview and in-depth and focused group discussions. As a result, future school principal hopefuls will benefit since they will be aware of the potential difficulties that may arise from holding the job. One can prepare for what to do and what not to do by just reading this study. Henceforth, this study contributes to future school leaders' learning and preparation.

Research Questions

1. What are the experiences of novice principals as fiscal managers?
2. How do they cope with the challenges or obstacles as fiscal managers?
3. What are the insights that can be drawn from this study?

Theoretical Lens

As a researcher, we took the time to check the theories that would be appropriate for this study and discovered one proposition and one idea. The first is the research of Butt, B.Z. (2010), implying that efficient implementation and adherence to financial management principles result in enhanced organizational performance. The second theory is an experiential theory, sometimes known as "learning by doing."

As mentioned, the study of Butt, B.Z. (2010) implies that optimal application and adherence to financial management methods lead to improved corporate performance. Companies that are well-managed financially are also operationally efficient. The improved performance that resulted in better quality posed a massive challenge for businesses (Butt et al. 2010). The proponent above clearly shows that, when handled correctly, financial management brings excellent improvements to a corporation's performance. The same goes for the schools: when the financial resources are well-managed, they will eventually have positive impacts, especially on the students and the school. This way, more stakeholders will be more interested in supporting the school after witnessing its development day by day. Hence, this could only mean that a school head should be literate enough to be a fiscal manager, as the school's performance is at stake.

Another theory is the experiential theory, which refers to learning through experience. According to David Kolb, this type of learning is "the process by which knowledge is formed through the transformation of experience, knowledge resulting from the combination of grasping and transforming experience" (Cherry, 2020). This theory takes a more holistic approach as it emphasizes how experiences like cognitions, emotions, and environmental factors influence the learning process. As a result, a new school principal should be fearless of new experiences because they will teach them, particularly about school finances.

As a result, Butt's (2010) proposition and David Kolb's theory are relevant to the study's success. Indeed, when the school head manages school finances well and correctly, it can positively impact the school. Moreover, school leaders should be confident in new experiences because they are also stepping stones to success.

Significance of the Study

This research bears significant inputs as it takes great skill and intelligence for someone to handle finances well. This is even evident in a global family set-up, where the root cause of some family problems is when a wife mishandles the finances or the husband cannot provide enough to meet the household's needs. In like manner, in a school context, fiscal management is a significant factor affecting school performance. So, as a school leader, one must be diligent in studying how to handle school resources well, as it may affect other school concerns.

Likewise, this study will directly benefit aspiring school leaders, particularly in their role as fiscal managers. This is also important in understanding the difficulties that new principals encounter. They may navigate the maze of financial decision-making by utilizing appropriate tools for better and sound decision-making, which may allow them to adapt various financial management competencies.

Future researchers will also benefit because they will see that not only the experiences of novice principals are being explored but also the fiscal manager of the school.

Definition of Terms

Travails – This refers to the struggles or challenges in a particular position
Novice School Principal – This refers to a leader of the entire school who is one to three years in service

Fiscal Manager – This refers to a person responsible for managing resources in an organization

Delimitations and Limitations

This study is qualitative-phenomenological, with six participants who are novice school principals in the Division of Davao City. The data were collected from the participants' emotions, viewpoints, and feelings through an in-depth interview and focus group discussion.

Further, this study only covers the school leaders who have been in charge for three years in service. Only individuals who have been school principals in a public school for three years or less are eligible to participate in our study. Also, this study does not focus on the experiences of school principals relating to the teachers or school personnel but on the financial management of the school resources.

Chapter 2

REVIEW OF RELATED LITERATURE

Travails of Novice Principals

The sharp transition from teaching to management is fraught with difficulties, causing anxiety since the new role is complex and involves immense responsibility; they need to alter their role perception and struggle to create an organizational culture complying with their vision (Khalid, 2017).

As the focus of change in the school is on the novice principals, who bring new expectations and hopes to each community (Flores, 2020),

Further, it cannot be denied that the challenges are significant, such as understanding what it means to lead the school and what needs to be done to improve (Beycioglu & Wildy, 2015).

Undoubtedly, it was discovered that novice principals have expectations regarding the extension of legal rights through new legislative arrangements, increased in-service training before starting as a principal, award and performance system innovations, sanctions against unfounded complaints, advanced activity for families, improved personal rights, and merit-based appointment assignment (Kara & Bilge, 2019).

Almost a third of the new principals said they were lonely in their job and felt as if they were responsible for running the entire school by themselves, with no help or supervision (Perestrelo, 2016).

On the sad part, there are a variety of reasons why principals choose to resign from positions for which they worked so hard, and unless there is enough support for them, there will be many turnovers because being the head of the school requires extra tasks (Bayar, 2016).

Moreover, school principals are responsible for a variety of management responsibilities and activities that have an impact on their effectiveness as school leaders, as they are also responsible for managing the entire school's educational, budgetary, infrastructural, and human resources in an ever-changing environment (Jinot & Balkooram, 2020).

Going on a survey discovered that new principals encounter various leadership challenges during their crucial first year as a principal. So novice principals need in-service and on-the-job professional training, such as mentoring, that enables them to face these leadership needs, as principals need to be mentored (Perestrelo, 2016).

The following statements are about concepts and contexts related to the difficulties of new principals:

Always Feeling the Need to Plan Ahead for School Improvement

A school improvement plan serves as a framework for bringing solutions to schools and aiding in closing the achievement gap. A strategy can assist us in developing and orchestrating a smooth road to exceptional results. It is helpful to imagine where we want our district to go and have fun devising a plan of action (Del Mar, -2021).

To make a step-by-step improvement plan, we must outline the steps necessary to attain this goal. Examples include allocating a budget for the people and equipment required for such a program, finding instructors who would work after school, ad selecting computer tools to facilitate ESL instruction (Bourg, 2020).

In the same way, most schools and districts plan, plan, plan, and then never study and believe that prediction should be included in planning since participants are more inclined to compare a new method to the projected outcome. Still, if the modification proposal works out differently than planned, there is much to learn (Schwartz, 2018).

Moreover, as with another critical takeaway from the planning chapter, we should create roadmaps rather than manuals mandating particular activities and arm individuals with the knowledge and resources they need to make better decisions on their own (Baldanza, 2018).

Difficulty in Addressing School Concerns Regarding School Resources

School districts worldwide are trying to find enough money to spend on resources in their classrooms, especially in high-poverty communities where schools struggle the most (Maffea, 2020).

Many school heads also claim that they lack the necessary skills in school finance and budgeting to fully engage in such conversations or advocate for increased school funding (Superville, 2019).

In addition, it agrees with this statement that when taking over our school's budget, it is easy to get bogged down by the numbers, but do not just be driven by how our school has budgeted in the past (Banning, 2018).

Also, schools need help managing their finances and keeping track of their fee collections and contributions even as they connect and engage students, parents, and alums to develop relationships and drive better achievement (Sriram, 2019).

Likewise, following the typical budgeting approach will almost surely result in inefficiency, and to be effective, the budgeting technique must be conducted in the correct order. (Hariharan, 2020).

Being Uncertain about the Factors to Consider in Handling School Finances

There are many factors to consider in handling school finances. Still, the very budgeting exercise has three primary goals: to create targets to inspire and reward performance, to coordinate resources by forecasting midterm financial results and planning appropriately, and to impose control by defining cost boundaries and centrally controlling cost allocation (Stange & Roos, 2020).

Moreover, uncertainty, in whatever form, illuminates a definite truth: businesses must tackle fluctuating business situations with agile planning, budgeting, and forecasting. Most companies, such as schools, even in steady times, need help with budgeting. Managers frequently spend too much time attempting to operate within a budget imposed on them (8020 Consulting Staff Writer, 2020).

On the other hand, prepare a budget knowing what will happen next. As we are not out of the woods yet making these challenging and, in some cases, controversial decisions, we should begin with the many data points we may already have in dusty folders or ancient spreadsheets. (Jordan, 2020)

Having Different Emotions as School Head

Stress is unavoidable for school leaders since the day-to-day grind of leadership is emotionally taxing, and new challenges and increased accountability produce a frenzy of feelings that may churn inside even the most influential leaders (Patti et al., 2018).

Adding on, it was observed that effective school administrators must recognize and handle their desire to lead and bring about school reform since their effect as school heads might be felt throughout the school and impact everything from the school's culture to the additional effort a student makes beyond what their teacher was willing to expend (Mason, 2018).

Further, a leader is an inspirational guide, someone to whom a group of people looks for confirmation and direction when faced with ambiguity or danger (Karakus et al., 2018).

Moreover, suppose our financial stress is extreme. In that case, it will have a detrimental impact on our mental and maybe even physical health because anxiety, sadness, behavioral changes such as withdrawal from social activities, and physical symptoms such as stomachaches or headaches can all result from financial stress (Scott, 2022).

Indeed, the growing expectations for accountability and educational reform put school administrators' duties under constant strain. Today, educational leadership is more emotionally appealing than task-driven since emotions and change are intertwined at the micro-level of organizational behaviors (Kareem & Kin, 2019).

In everyday life, secondary school leaders confront events that elicit emotion, such as leading through problems and understanding emotion following significant incidents. Self-reflection may help leaders better understand themselves, enhance communication, and prevent misunderstandings (Yamamoto et al., 2015).

Coping with the challenges or obstacles as fiscal managers

If we can lessen our money anxiety, we will be able to focus on other essential aspects of our life and relax, knowing that we have a strategy to deal with our financial condition (Caldwell, 2022).

And then, if we are feeling overwhelmed by financial stress, we should first calm ourself down since anxiety tends to rob us of our sense of self-control and our capacity to solve problems (Campbell, 2021).

Financial stress, in particular, is defined as emotional discomfort caused by money, and anyone who suffers from it is from a low-income household because they are more likely to experience it (Scott, 2022).

Indeed, as a budgeting exercise, it encourages us to ponder about how we spend our money since some bills may be able to be removed, and w we will not have to hustle to pick which invoices to pay first if we know which ones to pay first ahead of time (Renfro, 2021).

However, whatever our current circumstances may appear, there is a way out, as these tactics can assist us in breaking the pattern, relieving the stress of money troubles, and regaining stability (Robinson & Smith, 2021).

Collaboration with Mentors and Colleagues

Most of us have a favored method of cooperating with others, which impacts how our colleagues perceive us. Even cooperation in the virtual mentoring and social learning environment can significantly influence how a virtual group works and learns together to achieve goals (Browning, 2021).

Notably, mentoring is a procedure in which two or more people collaborate to advance a single person's career and talents and might be focused on a professional or personal setting (Goodyear, 2006).

Also, being a mentor is a critical job as it is not about demonstrating what to do to someone and demonstrating how our career shows the path people should go, but about guiding them through their career journey with comfort and support by assisting them in discovering their purpose (Burgé & Thiele, 2021).

Nevertheless, while one may learn a lot on their own, having a mentor is a genuinely significant benefit because this connection style allows for more in-depth, one-on-one learning about a new position (The Value of Mentorship, 2018).

In addition, collaboration is essential for mentoring, and maintaining mentor connections is also critical, so remain in touch and update them as required (Tsuruo, 2020).

Especially in the workplace, collaboration used to be restricted to in-person brainstorming and project coordination, but how we operate is evolving, particularly in how we collaborate (Vogel, n.d.).

Moreover, when it comes to professional collaboration, psychological safety is essential so that the team feels comfortable speaking out, as the more we grasp our colleagues' narratives about themselves—how they operate, where their competence rests, the obstacles they face daily—the higher their chances of working successfully with them will be (Maloney, 2020).

Continuous Learning and Updating

Continuous learning is the practice of constantly gaining new skills and information. This can take numerous forms, ranging from formal coursework to informal social learning, and it requires self-initiative and the willingness to face problems (Continuous Learning, 2022).

In particular, the only way to stay ahead is to keep learning and investing in ourselves, as this allows us to expand our skills and knowledge, stay current, and advance in our profession—or switch industries because continuous learning has also been demonstrated to boost morale, work satisfaction, and self-esteem (Sword, 2021).

The constant extension of knowledge and skill sets is referred to as "continuous learning" even in the workplace, which is frequently used in the context of professional development and is about obtaining new skills and information while simultaneously reinforcing what has already been taught (Chai, 2022).

In the same way, continuous learning is a professional development idea in which our staff is provided the chance to learn while working. It works best when the individual wants to learn and is ready to absorb new information (The Importance and Benefits of Continuous Learning, 2021).

Moreover, when it comes to keeping our best and brightest, a workplace that supports continuous learning is essential, especially if we provide those employees with opportunities for advancement while they remain with our firm. We may avoid the costs of attracting and training replacements (Rice, 2022).

On the other hand, when we change our job, personal life, community, and organization, lifelong learning is one of the most effective methods to deal with changes (Nagpal, 2017).

As with learning, which is necessary for survival, just like food nourishes our bodies, information and continued learning nourish our minds, as lifelong learning is an indispensable tool for every career and organization (Seven reasons why continuous learning is important, 2020).

Ingenuity and Resourcefulness

The idea of resourcefulness is to look at what is in front of us and optimize what we have to work with, as being inventive does not necessarily mean developing something new; it might simply mean making existing things operate better (Campbell, 2016).

However, when it comes to reaching professional goals, nothing beats ingenuity on the job because being resourceful at work, especially when we have set significant objectives, requires adopting a "will-do-at-any-cost" mindset and being willing to think outside the box to get the task done (McGrath, 2018).

In addition, as in school, ingenuity and resourcefulness are needed, even for Indian entrepreneurs and family companies, as they were dragged out of that age of poverty and hunger (Khanna, 2021).

Resourcefulness is a set of soft talents that includes problem-solving and creativity that may be used to solve professional issues as we broaden our skill set and demonstrate to employers that we are committed to their organization's success by being more resourceful (Indeed Editorial Team, 2022).

Furthermore, resourceful employees can develop solutions with limited resources, which is advantageous for any organization in any sector (Ariella, 2022).

Be Open and Optimistic

Being optimistic means having a positive attitude toward the world and believing that good things will happen and people's aspirations will be realized (Morin, 2022).

Similarly, it would be best to appreciate how much being optimistic and open-minded creates opportunities. (Mautz, 2021).

Significantly, optimism permits us to learn from mistakes, pick up the pieces, and go on to bigger and better things, as the most significant business ideas and times can be born from failure (Cutler, 2015).

Indeed, increasing our optimism may help us see people, circumstances, and work more positively, as optimists can lower their stress levels, increase their productivity, and have more meaningful experiences (Indeed Editorial Team, 2022).

Above all, a positive attitude has been scientifically shown to increase happiness and drive us to achieve our goals. If we deliberately attempt to appreciate the positive parts of our life, we will begin to notice silver linings under challenging situations (Calling All Optimists, 2020).

Further, optimism is a mental state marked by optimism and faith in achievement and a bright future because optimists anticipate positive results, whereas pessimists expect negative consequences (Scott, 2020).

Moreover, the first step in becoming more positive is to consider what our truly desire, which provides clarity and aids in prioritizing and strategizing (Umoh, 2017).

Adding on, optimists, by nature, do not sweat the minor stuff, as they not only produce less cortisol—the stress hormone—during difficult periods but also experience less perceived stress (Cassity, n.d.).

In fact, according to research, optimists have a lesser chance of developing impairments since they live a joyful life, so if we believe we are born pessimist who cannot think positively, this is only our mental process (Chatterjee, 2020).

That is why optimism is defined as the belief in the future and success of something or someone, as optimistic people focus on the positive aspects of a situation and believe that something good will happen (Kim, 2020).

On the other hand, negative thinking is viewed as a massive barrier. It also prevents individuals from reaching their full potential (The Importance of Optimism, 2020).

Act Our Role as School Head

A successful school head ensures that the teachers adopt the concept of academic achievement for everyone, and effective principals also promote ongoing professional development (Five Key Responsibilities, 2021).

In addition, following the devolution of responsibility, the head of the school will be the budget holder and financially liable for the school (in the first instance) (Head of School, 2013).

The principal's responsibilities include leadership, teacher assessment, and student discipline. Being a successful principal is difficult and time-consuming, and they balance the tasks given to them (Meador, 2019).

For this reason, we model the characteristics we want our employees to have. Even little activities, like where to have lunch, can allow us to model the behavior we want to see in our employees (Lee, 2020).

Of course, school leaders create and manage budgets for the school and ensure its financial stability because principals also collaborate with school board members and parents to disseminate any essential news or information about the school and its pupils (Principal job description, 2022).

Connect with our Mentors and Peers in the Field

Peer mentoring promotes a give-and-take relationship in which both workers provide advice, learn from one another, and grow professionally (Peek, 2022).

Undoubtedly, mentorship is a mutually beneficial professional relationship in which an experienced person (the mentor) passes on knowledge, expertise, and wisdom to a less experienced individual (the mentee) while also strengthening their mentoring abilities (D'Angelo, 2022).

Also, a peer mentor can provide someone else with direction, counsel, and support. They usually have more experience in the field or area than the mentee; however, this is only sometimes the case (Tina, 2022).

Furthermore, individuals can strengthen their leadership qualities through mentoring, as outstanding leaders can pass on their expertise and significant learnings to someone less experienced or ready to take on a leadership role (Cronin, 2020).

Be Literate in Fiscal Management

Financial literacy is the capacity to comprehend and effectively employ various financial abilities, including personal financial management, budgeting, and investing (Fernando, 2022).

So, even in some of the world's most sophisticated financial systems, a lack of financial literacy is a significant challenge that requires quick action (Lusardi, 2019).

That is why we need to improve our financial efficiency because perhaps there is a service that our team used to subscribe to but no longer utilizes. As we understand how each expenditure affects the balance sheet, it might be easier to discover strategies to save money (Cote, 2020).

Indeed, financially literate consumers not only handle money with more confidence but also have a better chance of dealing with their financial life's inevitable ups and downs by learning how to prevent and manage crises when they emerge (McGurran, 2021).

Budgeting is the foundation of effective financial planning because creating and adhering to a budget demonstrates how much money we have and where it is spent. Budgeting will assist us in identifying ways to conserve money and plan for the future (Madison, 2019).

Be Receptive and Updated on New Learnings

Avoid presuming that our answer is the only one and set aside time to connect with personnel and respond to their concerns (Lee, 2020).

Likewise, pretentious knowledge permanently blocks doors because the more we embrace this sensation of not knowing, the more room we make for inquiry (Udavant, 2020).

Indeed, everyone has innate tendencies—automatic responses that keep them in their comfort zone. However, relying too much on our natural attitudes might distort our perspective of the world since learning to extend into different mindsets broadens our range and assists us in determining the optimal reaction to the issue at hand (Franken, 2020).

Again, being receptive does not imply being open to all of the world's sounds since it is sometimes necessary to say no to distractions to focus on what is essential (Patrik, 2016).

Besides, people with a responsive attitude are more likely to be exposed to balanced information on all sides of an issue, pay equal attention to evidence supporting both viewpoints, and assess relevant arguments more equitably (Ordway, 2022).

Maintenance and Other Operating Expenses (MOOE)

The Department of Education is constantly improving its services to enhance the quality of teaching and learning results, and one of the reforms is the delegation of responsibility to schools for managing their operations and resources for school development to create an atmosphere conducive to continual improvement (Ochada & Gempes, 2018).

Further, allotments are released directly to Implementing Units (IUs) by the DBM offices, so the cash allocations matching the allowances granted are issued now by the DBM offices involved to the appropriate IUs' Modified Disbursement Scheme (MDS) Sub-Accounts (Llego, 2019).

Moreover, following the issuance of the corresponding guideline for the increase in capitalization threshold for a semi-expendable property by the Commission on Audit (COA), the Department of Education (DepEd) announced that the budget for Maintenance and Other Operating Expenses (MOOE) had been increased to P50,000 from P15, 000 (Hernando-Malipot, 2022).

Furthermore, submitting the MOOE liquidation report is a monthly activity of the schools in which expenses intended to improve the school facilities are charged. A correct and complete MOOE liquidation report results in the release of the cash advance intended for the MOOE of the following month (Llego, 2019).

To be more specific, the researcher included the MOOE liquidation report's school-based process or flow chart in the appendices.

Chapter 3

METHODOLOGY

This chapter describes how this research was done by the researchers, namely, Julie Ann D. Bayani and Dr. Eunice A. Atienzar. We gathered the details and ideas to produce a quality paper that would benefit future school leaders.

Research Design

Qualitative research gathers and evaluates non-numerical data such as text, video, or audio to better comprehend concepts, views, or experiences. It can be utilized to gain in-depth insights into a topic or to develop fresh research ideas. (Bhandari, 2020.)

Moreover, we used phenomenological qualitative design in our study. Phenomenology is qualitative research that examines an individual's lived experiences in the world (Neubauer et al., 2019). This can be used in this study, as it aims to explore the different experiences of novice principals as fiscal managers.

Role of the Researcher

As the researcher, we were responsible for designing, interviewing, transcribing, checking, reporting, thematizing, and analyzing this study. The actual interview, called a Focus Group Discussion (FGD), was done virtually via Google Meet and was video and audio-recorded after the topic was chosen. Field notes were used to enhance the documented evaluation. After the interview, the next step was to transcribe the recordings. The transcription was done verbatim for a simple and controllable approach to evaluating and investigating the information. We also classified the ideas in their comments and gained some additional insights due to our pressing on several critical issues. Since some comments were interlaced throughout the debate and interaction, labeling topics proved tricky, and the highlights of ideas had to be carefully gathered. The complexity of our job as a researcher centered on data analysis, where the data was coded, and each participant was issued a code, with aliases employed to conceal their identity. We needed to analyze the audio recordings for the thoroughness and accuracy of the presented ideas, concepts, and material. Where possible, we approached and exhaustedly sought clarifications from a few participants within our reach. The data was then analyzed, also known as "data mining."

Research Participants

This research was conducted among the six novice school heads. There were 11 prospective participants initially, but five declined for some reason. A sample of six to 20 participants is already sufficient (Ellis, 2016). Furthermore, we used purposeful sampling because it was widely used and well-known for identifying and selecting information—rich enough to comprehend the phenomenon under investigation and better instances relevant to the phenomenon of interest—from many sources. Participant selection is essential for this study because people are frequently questioned about their expertise and information. The choice of a purposive sample is critical to the quality of the data collected (Namey, 2007).

Two school principals attended the IDI. These principals serve at Davao City Division public schools for one to three years. They are between the ages of 30 and 58. Participants who have been in charge of a school for more than three years are not eligible. No sanctions were given to those who did not participate in the study.

Meanwhile, four school principals took part in the FGD. Because several factors may impact sample size in qualitative research, the concept of saturation should serve as a guiding principle (Mason, 2010). Similarly, they originated from the Davao City division of IDI. A homogeneous purposive sample was chosen for a shared attribute or set of traits (Crossman, 2020).

In FGD, the participants have less than three years of service and are school heads both in elementary and secondary public schools. Those who have more than three years of service are not included. Furthermore, those who were unwilling to participate in the study were not forced to answer the questions, and no sanctions were given either.

Data Collection

The novice school heads and principals were recruited personally, and we had to inform them well of the purpose of the interview as a condition of qualitative research. This happened after the approval of the permission letter I submitted to the Division office to conduct this study. Moreover, since face-to-face communication is still restricted, the participants were informed that the FGD would be done virtually at their preferred time. The same goes with the IDI, which will be done virtually as well, except with our school head, with whom we had the privilege of having an in-depth interview face-to-face since we are just in the same school.

In conducting the interviews for FGD and IDI, we used an online platform called Google Meet. As the researcher, we ensured that we established rapport at these moments and that they had no negative sentiments against the other participants or us. We also confirmed that the online meeting was recorded. This is why we were able to transcribe the information they provided precisely. Our data was obtained honestly and then analyzed.

Moreover, we are delighted with the results of both interviews. The participants may be few, but they are very rich in information, which they have saturated by answering mainly the research questions. Both interviews were conducted during their free period on Saturday, so we made sure to thank them with a token for devoting their valuable time to this study.

Data Analysis

The qualitative analysis aims to interpret the data and identify emerging themes to better comprehend the phenomenon under investigation. Meanwhile, data analysis is the process of gathering, modeling, and analyzing data to obtain insights that may be used to make decisions (Calzon, 2022).

After gathering the data, the next step is to classify it. The goal is to identify any patterns that indicate ideas that participants would convey during the data collection phase. Thematic analysis was used in this study to analyze the data acquired. The data were grouped into logical categories to summarize and provide meaning to the manuscript of notes. Specific codes were created to help us categorize the responses and detect emerging trends.

To familiarize ourselves with the data, we listened to the recorded interviews of the participants and transcribed them so that we could code the data afterward. We reviewed the data multiple times to familiarize ourself with the responses and readily recognize the common answers provided by the participants. Following that, we organized the typical reactions and discovered numerous themes.

Trustworthiness of the Study

We addressed the trustworthiness of our findings by implementing several ways to handle the four trustworthiness concerns that require consideration: credibility, dependability, conformability, and transferability (Shenton, 2004). The study's quality is determined by whether the data obtained are relevant and consistent. The credibility and objectivity of qualitative research can be increased by maintaining high credibility and impartiality.

We used the following techniques to address credibility: First, we became familiar with the participants' cultures before we began data collection. During the preliminary visits, this was accomplished. The study's goal was stated in letters issued to the heads of the schools. Second, we identified and contacted freshly hired school heads. Third, we used various strategies to ensure that the participants would provide accurate information for the study. The researcher must connect positively with the school heads to obtain the correct data.

Dependability, on the other hand, is a measure of the quality of the integrated data collection, data analysis, and theory production processes. To address the issue of dependability more directly, the study's methodologies were detailed, allowing a future researcher to repeat the work, albeit not necessarily to achieve the same outcome. As a result, the research design might be considered a prototype. Dependability is a criterion used to quantify trustworthiness in qualitative research. It also addresses the issue of uniformity. It would be best to determine whether the analytical procedure adheres to the acknowledged standards for a particular design. (Korstjens & Moser, 2018).

On the other hand, confirmability is needed to introduce impartiality and direct researchers to avoid bias. As a researcher, we ensured that all of the participants' comments and shared experiences were recorded. To attain confirmability, researchers must show that the findings are related to the conclusions in a way that can be understood, followed, and duplicated as a procedure. Its application significance is comparable to credibility, while confirmability has specific repercussions for research that makes policy recommendations (Moon et al., 2016).

Meanwhile, transferability is the capacity to transfer the outcomes of one set to another. This is critical for determining if the findings can be applied to other research projects. The study's findings and results might be used in various places, contexts, groups, and circumstances. We refer to this as "external validity" or "generalizability" in our introduction to study design. Readers notice the specifics of the study circumstance and compare them to the features of a place or condition they are familiar with in terms of transferability. If the two cases are sufficiently comparable, readers can deduce that the research results would be identical or similar in their situation. (Consultores, 2020).

Ethical Consideration

Ethical consideration is a set of ideas and beliefs that should be observed while dealing with others. Ethical principles ensure that no one acts destructively toward society or an individual. It prevents people and organizations from engaging in destructive behavior. Our whole study effort may be squandered if we fail to adhere to ethical principles. Our study time may be well-spent if we stick to all moral principles. The following are the ethical concerns that must be addressed while conducting the research project (Bhasin, 2020).

To develop respect for people, we requested Davao City's Schools Division Superintendent's permission to conduct our studies. We also followed the UMERCS procedure for research ethics. The participants were also asked to sign an informed consent form indicating their desire to participate in the study. The researcher owes the participants to respect them and not abuse their weaknesses.

Also, plagiarism is avoided by ensuring that the study contains no trace or evidence of distortion of someone else's work. Turnitin software was used to check the study for plagiarism.

To avoid fabrication, the study did not engage in any deliberate misreading of the task at hand. In evaluating and interpreting the results, the actual and original data from the study of the written interviews of the participants was used. It was the basis for collating the data based on the recording, note-taking, and responses to the questionnaires, avoiding fabrication.

This study did not include any misinterpretations to prevent work falsification. The ideas used and implemented are appropriate for the researcher's field of study. This is not an exaggeration.

The researcher adheres to the study's procedures to avoid a conflict of interest. There is no evidence of a conflict of interest in which a professional judgment relevant to the participants' primary interest of "welfare" is made. A secondary interest, such as financial, academic, or recognition, tends to influence the research's validity.

To establish goodwill, we requested their free time for an in-depth interview and their chosen location where they could openly share their views on the subject. Before the scheduled date and time of the in-depth discussion, each of them was given informed consent. Beneficence necessitates a commitment to minimize the participants' risks rather than maximize the rewards owing to them (Creswell, 2013). This research will be used to refine the newly formed schools. Their financial management competence will be enhanced, allowing them to become more effective school leaders.

In this study, deceiving the participants has no place. There was no evidence that the volunteers were misled about the possible harm.

We ensured that the newly-hired principals or school heads at the Davao City division could engage in this research of their own free will without any consequences, penalties, or loss of benefits. As a result, the study's goal and benefits will be explained to find schools that will participate. In addition, the participant's right to contribute to the body of knowledge was carefully evaluated and agreed on.

Furthermore, the author of this work is Julie Ann D. Bayani, a teacher at Communal National High School who also served as the researcher, as previously stated. Meanwhile, the co-author is Dr. Eunice Atienzar, who guided and supervised the completion of this paper.

Chapter 4

RESULTS

The results of the thematic analysis are presented in this chapter. Additional discussion is offered to clarify the themes and subthemes that emerged from the study's findings. Also, the results were generated through a computer software called NVIVO, and the screenshots are found in the appendices.

This table shows the profile of the participants. Four participants were for Focus Group Discussion (FGD) and two for In-Depth Interviews (IDI). Both IDD and FGD participants came from elementary and secondary schools of the division of Davao City.

Table 1

IDI and FGD Participants Profile

CODE	Pseudonym	Gender	Study Group	Age during Interview	Level
FGDPA-1	Ann	Female	FGD	35	Elementary
FGDPA-2	Liz	Female	FGD	40	Elementary
FGDPA-3	Omar	Male	FGD	40	Secondary
FGDPA-4	Jay	Male	FGD	30	Secondary
IDIPA-1	Jim	Male	IDI	45	Elementary
IDIPA-2	Joe	Male	IDI	58	Secondary

This table shows the experiences of novice school heads as fiscal managers. Four major themes were extracted from the answers of the participants in FGD and IDI from the questions in connection to the first objective of this study.

Table 2

Major Themes and Core Ideas on Experiences of Novice School Principals

or School Heads as Fiscal Managers

Major Themes	Core Ideas
Always Feeling the Need to Plan Ahead for School Improvement	Submitting request the soonest time possible for planning
	Having Simply too many Obligations to plan
	Adhering to the deadline to plan ahead
	Thinking of the school needs
	Following the process step by step planning
	Seeing the division office guidelines in accordance to the school goal
	Achieving school goals targeted for the year
	Rectifying the errors of past years to achieve goals
Having Difficulty on Addressing the School Concerns Particularly Regarding School Resources	There is no enough budget allocated for hauling and fare
	Very unfriendly to the schools in the far flung area
	Approval of the people involved or their signatories
	The delay of request
	Unfriendly systems for the aged school head
	Lack of training
Being Uncertain about the Factors to Consider in Handling School Finances	School Improvement Plan (SIP)
	Annual Procurement Plan (APP)
	Project Procurement Management Plan (PPMP)
	Comprehensive Timeline
	Transparency especially on the funds from stakeholders
	The understanding on the accountability of the school head
Having Different Emotions as School Head	Feel lucky since other teachers also help
	Blessed to have been helped
	Anxious on handling school funds
	Almost cried because the pressure is overwhelming
	Lonely being the sole administrator at their school
	Difficult feelings since dependent on PTA funds
	Quite happy because there is available school fund
	Shock with the rules and regulations of the DepEd
	Disappointed as there are no immediate actions

Always Feel the Need to Plan Ahead for School Improvement

"Pinaka importante na mga need sa school na-relay ra lang gyud sa PTA. So kaning para magkaroon ko ug fund lang gyud na magamit sa school kasi gina plano man gyud na nato to ahead no na na mao ni ang mga need sa school so kinanghanglan na pangitaan nato syag fund so at at a kaning the start of the school year naka plano na naka implement nako kung unsaon pag collect ang fund biski dili pa sya kinahangan" -Q1, FGDPA-3

"The most important is that the school's needs are relayed to the PTA. So, to have a fund that can be used in the school, we need to plan for these needs to be available before the school year starts. The ways on how to collect the fund should be implemented." -Q1, FG-DPA-3

"I think as a school head we need to plan tanan mga needed requirements especially sap ag request kasi meron syang mga step by step when you have the RCA or shall I say the request of cash advance." -Q1, FGDPA-4

"I think as a school head, we need to plan every needed requirement, especially in requesting because there is step by step when you have the RCA or, shall I say, the request of cash advance." -Q1, FGDPA-4.

Difficulty on Following the Guidelines and Policy Regarding MOOE

"Being a novice fiscal manager is difficult, especially with a very minimal budget in a newly opened school where resources are limited. I felt disappointed so many times that I wanted immediate action on my priority programs but could not implement it as I wanted them because of budgetary problems. I often resort to looking for stakeholders." –Q1, IDIPA-1

"I can say that it must be worked with hand and hand with both division and the school because mayroon din silang fault at fault dyan in a sense na matagal sya ma release ang kwarta that is why once mag mask na ng liquidation definetly at the end pa pud sya maliquidate sa isa ka school head. how to solve of that one maam no I think as a school head we need to plan tanan mga needed requirements especially sa pag request kasi meron syang mga step by step when you have the RCA or shall I say the request of cash advance." –Q1, FGDPA-3

"I can say that it must be worked for hand and hand with both division and the school since there is at fault in a sense that the release of the fund is long, and that is why once when the liquidation is asked, it will be done at the end of the deadline by the school head. *How to solve that one Maam, I think as a school head, we need to plan every needed requirement, especially about the request, because there is step by step when you have the RCA or, shall I say, the request of cash advance."* –Q1, FGDPA-3.

"But on the other hand, proper planning and implementation will somehow address the problem. Thus, clustered schools should work hand and hand to handle the finances properly with the help of the school planning and project team. "–Q1, IDIPA-1

"As a teacher, more on the academic side. As the school head, you are concerned about everything. The bulk of work is heavier when you are a school head as you focus on many things." –Q1, IDIPA-2.

Being Uncertain about the Factors to Consider in Handling School Finances

"Ang mga factors need nimo I consider syempre dapat kadtong mga SIP nimo imohang APP, PPMP dapat naka align na sya pareha namo karon ang amoang problema naa me gusto na ipabuhat however pag check diay namo sa APP pag pa canvass nako nya pag wala sya so isa jud diay to sa factor na dapat namo I work out" –Q1, FGDPA-1

"The factors that you need to consider are, of course, the School Improvement Plan (SIP), Annual Procurement Plan (APP) Project Procurement Management Plan (PPMP). Moreover, it should be aligned. Like our problem, we want something to be done, however when checked in our APP, when it was canvassed, and it is not found there (APP), so it is one of the factors that you need to work out." –Q1, FGDPA-1

"The factors that need to consider are the immediate needs of the school, the teachers, students, and the facilities.". –Q1, FGDPA-2

Having Different Emotions as School Head

"So how do I feel during my primary years kanang grabe jud nakahilak jud ko aning MOOE"-Q1, FGDPA-1

"So, how do I feel during my primary years? It was super I cried on this MOOE" –Q1, FGDPA-1

"Hmmm wala kaau nako na feel na kay tungod una wala man gud koy MOOE nga iliquidate ang pag start gyud amm while I understand ah na lisod gyud" -Q1, FGDPA-2

"Hmmm, I did not feel it that way (hard) since first I do not have the MOOE allocation to liquidate, and when we started, I did understand that it is going to be hard." -Q1, FGDPA-2.

"Noh regarding with the question no I want to state that the my experience handling the school fund is somewhat mix emotion in a sense that I am quite happy that because I have school fund however in terms of managing it in terms of the school projects it will be mix emotions to me since I am a newly hired school head so that is somewhat mix emotion lang maam jul, maybe later I could share a lot of experiences depending on the questions but as of the moment I could say that my feeling now is somewhat mix emotions especially handling school fund I've experience to have PTA collections since I started a school in a year 2020 and I also have MOOE in the same year so both I've experience PTA and MOOE and from that sense I can say that I happy yet sad sometimes shock with the rules and regulations in the department of education thank you and good afternoon." -Q1, FGDPA-4

"Noh, regarding the question, no, I want to state that my experience handling the school fund is somewhat mixed emotion in the sense that I am quite happy because I have a school fund; however, in terms of managing it in terms of the school projects it will be mixed emotions to me since I am a newly hired school head so that somewhat mixes emotion only Ma'am Jul, maybe later I could share many experiences depending on the questions, but as of the moment I could say that my feeling now is somewhat mixed emotions, especially handling school fund I have experienced to have PTA collections since I started a school in the year 2020 and I also have MOOE in the same year so both I have experienced PTA and MOOE, and from that sense, I can say that I happy yet sad sometimes shock with the rules and regulations in the department of education thank you and good afternoon." -Q1, FGDPA-4

This table shows how the novice school heads cope up with the challenges or obstacles as fiscal managers. There are four major themes which were extracted from the answers of the participants in FGD and IDI from the questions in connection with the second objective of this study.

Table 3

Major Themes and Core Ideas on How Novice School Heads Cope

with the Challenges as Fiscal Managers

Major Themes	Core Ideas
Collaboration with Mentors and Colleagues	Learn from your previous school heads now colleagues in the field
	Ask technical assistance or maybe from the division office
	Ask help from the Administrative Assistant (ADAS) because they are the ones who knows about the templates and everything that we need
	Regularly consult mentors to deal issues
	Must be assisted with the technical with the Public School District Supervisor (PSDS)
	Collaborate with your co-school heads
	Work with cluster MOOE Cluster Supervisor.

Continuous Learning and Updating	Plan ahead base on the school necessities and priorities
	Lay down right foundation for the position
	Increase in-service trainings
	Engaging in ne new learning as a first-time principal
	Watch webinar about on new handling MOOE
	Pursue professional and personal development
	Attend pre-program services for the job.
	Monitor the school movement
	Study fiscal management
	Hunger for more seminar on fiscal management
	Evaluate yourself often times
Ingenuity and Resourcefulness	Look for creative ways to improve the school
	Always initiate first on how to resolved payables
	List down several initiatives uplift self-courage
	Be hands on with the budgeting, accounting, procurement and asset management tasks
	Work with the parent community or the stakeholders
	Have a good accounting system for monitoring
	Write a promissory letter for your bills
Be Open and Optimistic	Believe that everything has a solution
	Develop positive working relationships
	Alter their role perception
	Understand the challenges to navigate well
	Emotional management
	Be transparent in the utilization of the school money
	Choose to look beautiful in the eyes of many
	Think you are the best visual aid for the teachers and the community so don't look haggard.
	Remember that this job is your bread and butter.
	Stop worrying as this does not help at all.
	Take partnership with your subordinates
	Be open to delegate tasks

Collaboration with Mentors and Colleagues

> *"There is a need to always connect to my mentors and colleagues because they can always guide and support me in many programs that will be implemented. I also believe that they are the best source of very nice feedback that can help me grow." Q2, IDIPA-1*

"One of my best practices to overcome the obstacles of being the school fund manager is talking and sharing the school's current situation with stakeholders."

- Q2, IDIPA-1

"One best practices namo is to really collaborate no especially sa amoang cluster head. At the same time blessed pud ko na naa koi isa ka teacher na kabalo na pud sya na mas hawd pud sya sa akoa sa paghimog request. Makahelp sya sa akoa sa liquidation kay before mu-rag gina akoa ra man gud nako tanan ana gud so bug.at man diay pag akoon nimo tanan. So you delegate dili pud I delegate tanan but you are partnering ba, ("Ma'am Jo unsa ni atoang kailangan buhaton unsa diay imong plano Ma'am"?). Naa lagi lagi mangutana sa akoa ana so happy ra pud ko na na a partnering and collaboration gyud with your teacher and your cluster." Q2, FGDPA-1

"One best practice that we have is to collaborate, especially with our cluster head. At the same time, I am also blessed since I have one teacher who knows and is now more expert in making a request. She is helping in the liquidation since I did it all before, and it is heavy that way. So you delegate, not that I delegate all, but you are partnering ("Ma'am Jo, what do we need to do, what is your plan, Ma'am"?). Some ask like that, so I am happy to partner and collaborate with my teacher and cluster." Q2, FGDPA-1

"Same thing with them delegation coordination and plan and monitoring and evaluation. So ako nalang gi kuan Jul gi isa isa, thank you." Q2, FGDPA-3

"Same thing with them delegation coordination and plan and monitoring and evaluation. So I just made it one Jul, thank you." Q2, FGDPA-3

"Sa department of education if you are a school head definitely you must be assisted with the technical with the PSDS in terms of the technical assistance or maybe from the division office to our education program supervisor or even in the regional office ana lang sya maam jul" –Q2, FGDPA-3

"In the Department of Education, if you are the school head, you must be assisted with the technical PSDS in terms of the technical assistance or maybe from the division office to our education program supervisor or even in the regional office, so it is like that, Maam Jul" –Q2, FGDPA-3.

"I agree with sir Jeson no of course our PSDS but and also my cluster MOOE cluster supervisor also sa mga people daghan jud kaau ug mga tao nga naka help sa akoa no and one of them also is my former school head sya pud ang isa sa nag recommend sa akoa na maging teacher in charge si Maam Doren Agliza Mendez and kanang mga principals pud na mas season, season principals and even us kami na mga peers no kami diri sa cluster six mag tinabangay me so mao na sya ang mga tao na nakapa help sa amoa na to really manage our school kung unsay mga problema kami ra puy mag sinumbungay ug kami ra puy mag tinabangay." –Q2, FGDPA-1

"I agree with Sir Jeson, of course, our PSDS and also my cluster MOOE Cluster Supervisor. Also, the people and so many people helped me, and one of them is my former school head. He also recommended me to be a teacher in charge, Ma'am Doren Agliza Mendez, and the other principals who are more seasoned, and even us, the peers here in cluster six. We helped each other, and so these are the people who helped us to manage our school on whatever problems, we are the ones who talk to each other about it and help each other." –Q2, FGDPA-1

"Okay pagkakaron ang nakita nako na mag help sa akoa isa kaning ADAS kay sila man ang nakabalo sa kanang mga templates tanan tanan mga gamiton and of course ang property custodians. So far sa akong estado karon maam mao pa na sila aside from sir jeson nga permenente jud na sila naa dira and maam joana and sir marlon sangpiton lang jud na biski pa alas onsi sa gabie tubag jud na sya dayon." -Q2, FGDPA-2

"Okay, as of now, I see that the one who helped me is one of the ADAS because they are the ones who know about the templates and everything that we need to use and, of course, the property custodians. So far, in my situation now, they are the ones aside from Sir Jeson who are always there and Ma'am Joana and Sir Marlon whom I call even at 11:00 p.m., he will answer right away." -Q2, FGDPA-2.

"My previous school heads and my new co-school heads in the district where I am assigned." Q2, IDIPA-1

Continuous Learning and Updating

"webinar katong about sa new handling sa MOOE kato sya jul. Pero mostly man gud hands on man jud sa hands on dinha jud ka maka learn . kay usahay dili kaau ko kasabot sa webinar pero pag abot na sa ano sa pagsulbad sa problema kay anaon diay na sya naa diay pina anaon ra diay to. Kay taas kaau sila iexplain so mas makalearn ko sa hands on siguro ana pud ko na learner." –Q2, FGD-PA1

"Webinar about new handling MOOE, that is it Jul. Nevertheless, mostly is hands-on, it is hands-on, and there you can learn because sometimes I do not understand the webinar, but when it comes to solving the problem, you would realize it is just like that. It is very long to explain, so I learn more perhaps on hands as I am like that kind of a learner." –Q2, FGD-PA1.

"Same thing with them Jul, I've attended latest seminar regarding a with resources but for me kung enough ba sya or dili sya enough. Dili sya enough pa since naa pa me sa 3 years and below pa me halos tanan sa amoang kuan jud sa amoang experience so hopefully looking forward for more seminars regarding with regading on how to handle resources, thank you." –Q2, FGDPA-3

"Same thing with them, Jul, I have attended the latest seminar regarding resources, but if it is enough, it is not. It is not enough since we are still in three years and below, all of us in our experience so hopefully looking forward for more seminars regarding how to handle resources, thank you." –Q2, FGDPA-3.

"Seminar, it's part of the requirement kasi so you need to know the basics let's start the basic. So as mentioned noh SIP is the road map for 3 years sa school 2-3 years or 3-4 years ana sya. So SIP would be your stating board as to looking for if you want to be equip in school resources kasi you need to have funds noh kanang school improvement plan so as to kuan pud and then actually all the school heads were kanang were given a chance to have a training. Yung mga new mga untrained school heads for k-12 program so part of it I'm sure that there will be topic on school resources how to handle school finances." -Q2, FGDPA-4

"Seminar, is part of the requirement because you need to know the basics, so let us start the basic. Also, as mentioned, SIP is the road map for three years of the school, 2-3 years, or 3-4 years. So SIP would be your starting board to look at if you want to be equipped with school resources because you need funds. Moreover, part of the school improvement plan is that the school heads were given a chance to have training. The new untrained school heads for K-12 program so part of it I am sure that there will be a topic on school resources on how to handle school finances." -Q2, FGDPA-4

"I have attended MOOE Seminars: Seminars for Untrained School Heads" -Q2, IDIPA-2

Ingenuity and Resourcefulness

"If I am going to gauge my accomplishment in addressing school concerns, I say that I had fulfilled 65% of our annual implementation plan. It was because of the hindering factors experienced, especially with these trying times." -Q2, IDIPA-1.

"As to what extent were you able to explore in addressing school concerns kuan pa sya kanang dili pa gyud kaau nako kanang nahimo ang tanan or or pasabot wala pa gyud nako na explore ang tanan Nakong pwedi himoon to address school concern. As of karon maam kay gamay pa man ang amoang problem kana bang ang pag address nako sa mga concerns nako sa school is kanang tung kutob sa akong nahimo palang wala pa ko nag go beyond sa uncomfortable zone. Kumbaga naa pako sa akong comfort zone in addressing school concerns. Siguro tungod siguro kay bag.o pa maam". Q2, FGD-PA2

"As to what extent were you able to explore in addressing school concerns, it is just not that I have done everything or I mean I have not explored everything yet to address school concern. As of now, ma'am, we only have a few problems, and it seems like I address school concerns to the best that I can, but I have not gone beyond the uncomfortable zone yet. I am still in my comfort zone in addressing school concerns. Perhaps because we are still new." Q2, FGD-PA2

"So everytime na muaabot na gyud ug 2 months ang amoang electricity murag ma panic ko. Mapressure ko ba kay dili nako gyud gusto mahitabo sa akoang time na maputlan ang skwelahan ug kuryente. So since wala pa man ang amoang request ay wala pa man ang amaoang budget niabot so tapal sa jud ana lang gyud. So hopefully ingon man sila Sir Arvie(accounting) na ma-reimburse lang man sya. So ana gyud ang atoang accountability no

kanang unta naa kwarta jud unta dapat ang school head kay para dali ra kaau ikatapal ba ana pero sige lang kay God will provide lang man gihapon." –Q2, IDIPA-1

"So every time that the bill reaches two months, I will go into a panic. I get pressured because I do not want it to happen like the last time we disconnected from our school's electricity. So since our budget has yet to be approved, I will be the one to pay it first. So hopefully, it will be reimbursed as Sir Arvie (accounting) said. So that is our accountability, hoping that every school head has spare money to pay it first. Anyhow, God will provide. –Q2, IDIPA-1

"Soliciting from stakeholders and going to other places for this matter." –Q2, IDIPA-2

Openness and Positivity

"Yes, delayed MOOE will certainly affect the priority needs of the school, but with the extending arms of our stakeholders, I am always optimistic that we can still deliver. by looking for stakeholders to help realize the school's optimum goals." Q2, IDIPA-1

"We don't have any choice man but to look beautiful in the eyes of many man gyud no. Lain pud kaau Jul no na you are the head you are the best visual aid for the teachers and the community yet kuan kaau ka tan.awon haggard. Mao lang jul as If lang na nothing happens mao lang jud sya ang imong buhaton no. Pero behind that happiness, behind that success or behind that smile there are a lot of kuan no pinagdaanan nimo nga challenges ive experience na nakaaway gyud nako akong accountant. Ang giingon sa akoa kay among all the school na iyang na meet ako daw nag pinakapamati and I don't care kay mali man pud gud to iyahang point kasi dili man gud sya pwede gud jul na I change rag kalit ang imohang request it is because lahi ang na release na kwarta, ako jud ang mo adjust, so murag ing. ana gud sya. Pero wala tay mabuhat kundi go work lang gihapon kay naa man sa system no bread and butter man nato sya. Unless kung business man ko, dugay nako nihawa but we still love I chose to still love my work in the department of education." -Q2, FGDPA-3

"We do not have any choice, of course, but to look beautiful in the eyes of any man. It is not good, Jul, that you are the school head, you are the best visual aid for the teachers and the community, yet we look haggard. Just that Jul, as if nothing happens, that is what you will do. However, behind that happiness, success, or smile, there are many challenges that I have experienced to the point that I argued with the accountant. I was told that I am the only school head who got the greatest pride, and I do not care because it is also wrong that the request will be changed in a snap just because the money released is different; it seems like I will be the one to adjust and it is like that Jul. Moreover, we can do nothing about it but keep on working since the system is already there, and this is our bread and butter. Unless I am a businessman, I would have left the post already, but we still love, I still love my work in the education department." -Q2, FGDPA-3.

"How do I remain optimistic in this kind of situation? Kanang ano lang gyud kanang salig lang ko mao gyud na akoang sig isip na masulbad lang gyud tanang problem ana sagubangon sa skwelahan. Kay if I keep on worrying wala man gihapon ma help akong pag worries so I

pray na lang nako na I help ko sa Ginoo. Ay isa siya na sa akong gina pray perme ug pina-ka importante gyuda na prayer para sa akoa is hatagan jud ug wisdom kay ang knowledge man gud sometimes dili gyud nato masaligan no pero if its wisdom from the Lord especially if kanang mga lisod na mga problema na mura mag tama pero dili mani tama. Murag ana gud, so you need to really pray for wisdom and to trust na everything will be okay all is well. –Q2, IDIPA-1

"How do I remain optimistic in this kind of situation? It is like you believe that I always think everything will just be solved, the school's problem. Because if I keep on worrying, it does not help at all, so I just pray to God instead. Moreover, the one I always prayed for is the most important- to receive wisdom and knowledge since sometimes we cannot depend on anything but the wisdom that comes from the Lord, especially in difficult problems, as it seems right but not. It is like that, so you need to pray for wisdom and trust that everything will be okay as well." –Q2,IDIPA-1.

"Wala gyud kay choice as a school head diba no? Basta leader gyud ka mam wala gyud na na Kuan kanang unsay tawag ani naa pa ba kay wa gyud kay choice. Sa in the middle sa negative kanang negative na situation kung ang tanang negatibo ikaw na lang gyud magpa-biling optimistic." Q2, FGDPA-1

"You have no choice as a school head, right? If you are the leader Ma'am, it is nothing. You call it as if there is no choice. In the middle of the negative situation, if all are negatives, you will remain optimistic. "-Q2, FGDPA-1.

"I compose myself by thinking of a solution like getting from other sources like PTA that is readily available." Q2, FGDPA-1

This table shows the insights that can be drawn from this study given by novice school heads as fiscal managers. Four major themes were extracted from the answers of the participants in FGD and IDI from the questions in connection to the third objective of this study.

Table 4

Major Themes and Core Ideas on Insights that Participant Can Share

to Their Peers and the Academe in General

Major Themes	Core Ideas
Act Your Role as the School Head	Improve personal rights
	Be the initiator
	Be prepared for the management technicalities
	Create an organizational culture related to school's vision
	Develop unique voice as leader
	Confront with grace the oppositions
	Accept various management responsibilities
	Face leadership needs
	Manage time well and appropriately
	Take responsibility on fiscal management
	Observe appropriate and favorable procedures
Connect with your Mentors and Peers in the Field	Maintain and develop positive professional relationship
	Ask help to face and interact several elements of issues
	Seek mentor's help to deal with various issues
	Look up to those mentors with more experiences
	Win new staff's trusts
	Form a dedicated procurement team

Being Literate in Fiscal Management	Be budget conscious
	Evaluate budget
	Do not separate yourself from others
	Account school's money regularly
	Get good accounting systems which entails storing data
	Make sure it is the basis for decision making
	Observe and acknowledge lack of financial resources
	Have always and integrity in handling public finances
	Attend enhanced program on fiscal management
	Goal to succeed in developing fiscal management plans
	Understand its technicalities
	Keep balance on managing school financial resources
	Use another source of funding such as PTA und
	Get effective school finance officers
Be Receptive and Willing to Learn	Willing to attend seminars and trainings
	Bring as well new initiatives for the school improvement
	Adopt digitalized education
	Be knowledgeable on dealing the numerous school demands
	Attend in-service service webinar/seminars and trainings
	Join an induction program for school principal
	Integrate succession plans
	Manage information differently
	Learn new systems
	Don't hesitate to receive new ideas even from subordinates

Act Your Role as School Head

"How do I establish my authority ano jud sya you need to walang personalan lang ingana gud walang personalan kasi shes just my friend for the longest time pud I consider her as my friend and katong pagabot na na naging school head nako lahi maam lahi na akoang concerns ana gud so I need kailangan jud ko na as a leader … then I could establish my authority so as long as wala koi ginaapakan nga tao and naga sunod lang pud ko sa mga deped orders." -Q3, FGDPA1

"How do I establish my authority, is like you need to think not of personal issues even if she is my friend that I have considered for the longest time. When it comes to me as a school head, it is different concerns, so I need to stand as a leader, and then I could establish my authority as long as I do not step on other people's rights and I am also just following the DepEd orders." -Q3, FGDPA1.

"Ako kuan siguro pinakauna dapat as kaning fiscal manager kanang ikaw ang mag initiate no" -Q3, FGDPA2

"As for me, perhaps first as a fiscal manager, I should be the one initiating" -Q3, FGDPA2.

"Same thing to the initiator, and you should act as the leader rather than being a manager because a leader knows how to listen and communicate with the members and at the same time follow what is right and must.be guided with the legal basis base on the answer of ma'am. Thank you."-Q3, FGDPA3

"Try to follow your job description and learn from the mistakes." -Q3, IDIPA2.

Connect with your Peers and Mentors

"I believe that no one on an Island. Thus, connecting with peers and mentors is crucial in gaining more knowledge. The experiences of my mentors and peers will somehow guide me to better decision-making." -Q3, IDIPA1.

"Very important (to connect with mentors and colleagues) because there is no such thing word, monopoly meaning monopoly of the knowledge and skills of leading people or handling a school. So, I love asking my peers and my friends about certain tasks and how to do them. What I am going to do for me to submit a certain report and handle a school." -Q3, FGDPA3.

"One of my best practices to overcome the obstacles of being the school fund manager is talking and sharing the current situation of the school to stakeholders." -Q3, IDIPA-1

"As a leader school leader kani struggle kaau nako ning mag connect kay personality nako kay dili ko ka ing.ana ka outgoing maam ba. So siguro mao siguro kanang para sa akoa it's a call kay kabalo ko sa akoang kaugalingon nga dili ko ingon ana in which pag leader ka imoha gyud na syang himoon. So importante kaau mag connect because there are a lot of things na sa imong huna huna sakto pero sa legally technically dili diay sya sakto." -Q3, FGDPA2

"As a school leader, that is my struggle to connect since my personality is not outgoing, Ma'am. So maybe this is a call for me, for I know in myself that I am not like that, which as a leader, you should do (to connect). So it is essential to connect because there are many things that in your mind are correct but legally and technically are not." -Q3, FGDPA2.

"Knowing their experiences and being mentored by peers is a good step toward learning the processes and to better fiscal management." -Q3, IDIPA1.

Being Literate in Fiscal Management

"Very important gyud sya kay diba mao to akong ingon na ikaw man gyud...Gipahimo nimo sa uban pero pagmagkamali na ikaw man gihapon ang accountable, so dapat ikaw gyud mismo kabalo jud ka sa process and mao ng usahay mag hands-on gyud ko sa mga dapat buluhaton. As school head although naa man gyuy time na edelegate nako no pero katong mga basic na dapat gina trabaho sa school head dapat literate ug kabalo gyud ta sa process.-Q3, FGDPA-1

"It is important since it is you. You allow others to do it, but in the end, if there is a mistake, you are still the accountable person. That is why you should know the process yourself, so sometimes I am very hands-on with what things to do. As a school head, although there are times that I will delegate the task to others but to the basic task of the school head, I should be literate about the process." - Q3, FGDPA-1

"Anyway kuan sya very significant why because you are the head you are the hope of the entity. You are the head of the procurement entity so if we will talk about fiscal management meaning accountability and transparency wise sa imoha man sya tanan so for me significant kaau say jul mao lang to thank you." -Q3, FGDPA-3

"It is very significant because you are the hope of the entity. You are the head of the procurement entity, so if we talk about fiscal management, accountability and transparency are everything on you. So for me, it is very significant Jul. thank you." -Q3, FGDPA-3.

"As a school head, it is very significant since you are the final say to the good of the school." -Q3, IDIPA-2.

Be Receptive and Updated on New Learnings

"Siguro ako lang ang wla kasabot nga ing.anaon lang diay na siya pero as of karon murag what are the learning programs that they could be handling school resources training mga training sa SIP mga ingon ana kay dira man gud ang pag handle man gud sa resources depende sa imong plano and ang tanan man gud na resources naka kuan sya naka anchor sya sa imong SIP which is actually SIP is kaning unsay tawag ana kanang imohang plan imohang vision man pud gud sya. Murag ana ba wala kaau ka nag hisgot didto ug kanang sa SIP wala kaau ka nag hisgot ug kwarta did2 pero pag imo syang I breakdown ang ending niya kay kwarta murag ana ba resources ang kinahanglan para ma achieve nimo tung imohang plan didto imohang improvement plan ana." -Q2, FGDPA-2

"Maybe I am the only one who does not understand yet that it works that way. However, as of now, it seems like the learning programs could be handling school resources training on School Improvement Plan (SIP), something like that since handling resources depends on your plan and all resources are anchored to your SIP since it is your plan and your vision. It seems like, in SIP, the money thing is not mentioned, but when you have to break it down, the ending is money like the resources needed to achieve the plans, there is where your improvement plan be at." -Q2, FGDPA-2.

Chapter 5

DISCUSSION

This part of the study presents a discussion of the results of the study. Each theme generated for each qualitative question/ objective of the study is explained with literature citations.

Below are the generated major themes which answer the first research question: What are the experiences of novice principals as fiscal managers?

Always Feel the Need to Plan Ahead for School Improvement

To achieve every goal, there should be plans to make. In management, planning is determining actions to achieve a goal, anticipating changes and obstacles, and determining how to employ the best human resources and opportunities to achieve the desired end (Anastasia, 2019).

Even the famous writer, philosopher, scientist, and politician in the name of Benjamin Franklin says, "If you fail to plan, you are planning to fail" (Ciperski, 2020). Having said that, once you miss out on planning, do not expect success. Hitting the target needs severe action plans.

Difficulty in Following the Guidelines and Policy Regarding MOOE

Guidelines and policy are two important things when trying to attain a specific objective. In this regard on MOOE, there are many on the list that some school heads find challenging to follow. However, it is good that both offices in the Central and Division innovate online systems now and then. However, as long as some cannot follow, these systems still need to be improved (Getahun, 2018).

When individuals struggle to follow instructions, the effects are apparent: things either do not get done or get done poorly. However, people may suffer in mysterious or unrelated ways (Morin, 2022).

Being Uncertain about the Factors to Consider in Handling School Finances

There are factors to consider in handling school MOOE as mentioned by the participants, such as School Improvement Plan (SIP), Annual Procurement Plan (APP), and Project Procurement Management Plan (PPMP). These are the documents a school head should be hands-on and knowledgeable about. Nevertheless, sometimes, they become uncertain about these factors, and when uncertainty is encountered, the brain is easily pushed to overreact (Webb, 2020).

In addition, being a school head is challenging, especially when you are uncertain of some things, particularly in your novice years, as reiterated by Villoria et al. (2021) that the difficulties that novice school principals face include school and curriculum restructuring, accountability requirements, and changing municipal initiatives. The interaction of these several elements causes some inexperienced school principals to resign during their third year.

Having Different Emotions as School Head

It is common for people that when introduced to or encountered new things, different emotions mixed up. An in life, like our emotions, is not necessarily linear. We constantly handle numerous emotions all the time (Witkin, 2019).

It should be noted as well that these individuals, as beginners in the position, struggle and get frustrated with what they are expecting as it was discovered that novice principals have expectations regarding the extension of legal rights through new legislative arrangements, increased in-service training prior to starting as a principal, awards and performance system innovations, sanctions against unfounded complaints, increased training for families, improved personal rights, and merit-based appointment assignment (Kara, & Bilge, 2019).

Below are the generated major themes which answer the first research question: How do they cope with the challenges or obstacles as fiscal managers?

Collaboration with Mentors and Colleagues

Honestly, as the saying goes, no man is an island, which is so true in this study. This remarkable statement means that no one in this world can exist alone since we all require a community or a group of people to have a better life (Aparna, 2018). Participants who are the school heads may already be very skillful and knowledgeable at this level, but they still recognize the need to collaborate with a mentor and colleagues.

Undoubtedly, the feeling of isolation and loneliness can be exacerbated by the fact that principals are frequently the sole administrators at their schools. In many cases, the next closest school is so far away that opportunities for face-to-face collaboration with other principals are limited. Some people experience such intense feelings of alienation, isolation, and loneliness that they consider quitting their jobs. The best predictor of a new principal's departure from the profession is isolation (Bauer & Silver, 2018).

Continuous Learning and Updating

It is only possible to improve the school with the continuous learning and updating of the school head. It is often known as "upskilling," consistently picking up new skills and knowledge over time (Sword, 2021). It should be the school head's sole responsibility to be learning and updating about the system, particularly in handling financial matters. This way, the subordinates looking up to them will understand.

Accountability pressures (the pressure to boost test scores, for example) were listed as the most often expected obstacles by principals (Swen, 2019). So with this kind of pressure, a school head must learn and update continuously.

Ingenuity and Resourcefulness

Knowledge alone will never be enough for any position, especially as a school head. Being resourceful means the capacity to identify and use available resources to address issues and accomplish objectives (Lee, 2018). Of course, this comes along with ingenuity, allowing an absurd notion to develop into something genuinely brilliant (McGrath, 2018). Hence, as the organization's leader, we are responsible for finding ways to meet its needs.

That is why some schools supplement their income from other sources by soliciting funds from educationally engaged organizations, such as parents and communities, through fundraising events. They can also get help through social cooperation funds, such as local banks, USA-Aid, and UNESCO grants (Chonjo, 2018).

Openness and Positivity

The financial matter is a big deal to every organization, particularly in school. Thus, the school heads cannot afford to be negative on this issue. Positive thinking and being willing to accept assistance from others make us stronger and improve our sense of connection to the world we live in (Coutinho, 2020).

Furthermore, principals make money management a group effort. In their respective schools, all principals formed financial management committees (FINCOM). The FINCOMs are teacher representatives, governing body parents, and the treasurer and chairpersons of all other school committees. Other committee chairpersons are included to ensure that budgetary decisions are sensitive to the expectations and requirements of various groups within the school to ensure openness (Myende, et al 2018).

Below are the generated major themes that answer the first research question: What insights can be drawn from this study?

Act Your Role as School Head

As a school head, one should know the authority he/she has, especially when it is according to the constitution as it is written in Republic Act 9155, also known as the Governance of Basic Education Act, provides that a school must be directed by a school head who has "the authority, responsibility, and accountability for achieving higher learning outcomes," (Macadatar, 2020). Knowing this, a school head will have solid confidence to act on his/her role.

Moreover, we frequently avoid situations or individuals that hurt us when it comes to developing personally and as leaders. Furthermore, frequently, the very thing we want to avoid is the same thing that will propel us into more incredible growth and development (Dickerson, 2022). That is why, instead of resisting the opposing subordinates, learn and grow from them.

Connect with your Peers and Mentors

A mentor is a person who can offer you friendship and life advice. It is optional for them to have experience in the specific career route they intend to take. No one is above or below us, regardless of our age, whether we are 23 or 63. Recognize that we each contribute equally, though not in the same ways, as we foster these relationships. We may acquire knowledge and improve each other's talents by establishing connections with people at similar career stages (Ochieng, 2022).

Moreover, mentors can play a crucial role in helping new principals gain confidence, enhance their management skills, and establish themselves as instructional leaders. Also, having a mentor helps people perform better, rise professionally more quickly, and even like their jobs more. Mentors also gain from this. "To teach is to learn twice," after all (Horoszowski, 2020).

Being Literate in Fiscal Management

Taking one step forward in a particular task is easier if we are literate. Being financially educated helps a person to be better prepared for certain financial hurdles, which reduces the likelihood of personal economic suffering (CFI Team., 2021). Hence, it is vital to be literate as a school leader in fiscal management as we hope to commit few mistakes to none regarding this matter.

Adding on, there were proposed enhancement programs on school fiscal management to enrich administrators' and teachers' knowledge and awareness relative to the financial aspects. This recommendation was drawn from the study of Mahumot, G. (2022), a teacher from DepEd, since he found out that there is no significant relationship between teacher morale, the school's financial management, and organizational climate.

Be Receptive and Willing to Learn

As a school leader, one has to be willing to receive new learnings on the whereabouts of the system itself. This way, the danger in handling school finances is lesser than expected as they understood and by the correct process. Thus, training and seminars help as technology and current work approaches do not stand still, and we should not. We indicate that we are a bright and essential addition to the team by exhibiting our willingness to enhance our abilities, staying on top of industry trends, and consistently increasing our expertise (Schooley, 2022).

In addition, the government should provide in-service training and workshops on financial resource management for heads of public secondary schools to learn how to manage school funds successfully (Edmund & Lyamtane, 2018).

Implication for Educational Practice

Based on the findings of this study, these are the following implications I was able to draw out the:

In a dynamic educational system, every school is perceived to improve each year, primarily in the school leader. Being able to lead people is already good, but it continues as many factors need to consider, such as fiscal management. As mentioned repeatedly in this study, finances significantly affect school performance. Moreover, if there is a lack of support for the school heads in every aspect, the school's performance may be put at risk.

Since new principals are still learning to adapt to their new environment, it is very likely that their methods of performing assigned tasks, such as fiscal management, will be less effective when compared to seasoned principals. It is worth noting that they should refrain from shelling out from their pockets regarding school expenses, as this is way too much. Aside from they find it hard to learn new tasks, they also need to double their effort in finding resources whenever the budget still needs to be available. This would cause them much time, and when they feel tired, they need help to do the job effectively. Sometimes, skipping the necessary tasks would be the best option. This can make them doubt their ability to lead and become good leaders. Thus, the higher office must be able to ensure that there will be enough budget for every school every day. Otherwise, this can negatively impact the school's performance as a whole. On the other hand, it is good to know that according to the Department of Education, the maintenance and other operating costs (MOOE) threshold for public schools has been raised to P50,000 as a result of a new provision included in the 2022 General Appropriations Act (GAA) (DepEd). "This provides more freedom for DepEd's schools and offices to directly acquire printers, computers, tablets, and other vital goods to aid in their daily operations and classroom instruction," the department said in a statement (Cruz, 2021).

Furthermore, a lack of support from their superiors and colleagues can significantly impact their performance. As mentioned in the previous chapter, superiors and peers of novice school heads play an essential role in their personal and professional development. The lack of seminars and training, mentoring, and exposure to the experiences of the senior principals can make them feel unworthy to be called leaders. Not only did the newly hired principals need help with superior and peer support, but they also faced opposition from subordinates. This experience may make it more difficult for them to assist the school in improving. It can even obstruct the goal of instilling quality learning in students, especially if they are bombarded with additional tasks and roles that are added to their duties and responsibilities.

Implication for Future Researchers

Future researchers should build on the findings of this study and provide the audience with a broader source of information about the skills and competence of newly hired principals in the current educational setting.

The researcher also recommends that aspiring school heads in the future not just depend on the given training and seminars. However, be self-sufficient so that we are unstoppable in achieving our school success goals, especially when we cannot find support from anyone.

Concluding Remarks

The researcher's path in this study was not easy, but there are no regrets because there were many learnings along the road. We have realized that mentorship, training, and attitude are essential in this position. Lastly, we have learned that being a principal at a public school, like being a teacher, is a noble career. Most of them may be overwhelmed by the different tasks. However, the joy of achieving every objective for school advancement cannot be compensated by any amount that other professions may offer.

REFERENCES

Anastasia, (2019). How to succeed with planning in management and why it is important. Retrieved from https://www.ringcentral.com/gb/en/blog/planning-in-management/.

Aparna, (2018). No man is an island. Retrieved from https://importantindia.com/ 29294/no-man-is-an-island-essay/.

Ariella,S. (2022). The most important resourcefulness (with examples). Retrieved from https://www.zippia.com/advice/resourcefulness-skills/.

Baldanza, M. (2018). Rethinking school improvement: planning with purpose and living with plan. JustAsk Publications & Professional Development. Retrieved from https://justaskpublications.com/just-ask-resource-center/e newsletters /professionalpractices/rethinking-school-improvement/.

Bhandari, P (2020). What is qualitative research? methods & examples. Retrieved from https://www.scribbr.com/methodology/qualitative-research/.

Bourg, C. (2020). What is a purpose of a school improvement plan?. LSU Online and Continuing Education. Retrieved from https://online.lsu.edu/newsroom/articles/ what-purpose-school-improvement-plan/.

Browning, C. (2021). Collaboration styles for mentees, mentors, advisers and others. mentorcliQ. Retrieved from https://www.mentorcliq.com/blog/4-collaboration- styles-in-social-learning.

Burgé, G. & Thiele,B. (2021). How can mentors and mentees work together for meaningful collaboration? Retrieved from https://www.prdaily.com/how-can- mentors-and-mentees-work-together-for-meaningful-collaboration/.

Caldwell, M. (2022). 5 Strategies to deal with financial stress. *The Balance is part of the Dotdash Meredith publishing family.* Retrieved from https://www. thebalance.com/dealing-with-financial-stress-2385957.

Calling All Optimists. (2020). The benefits of a positive mindset. Retrieved from https://www.callingalloptimists.com/the-importance-of-optimism-during- challenging-times/.

Campbell, A. (2021). Financial stress: what's money go to do insanity?. Better Up. 1200 Folsom St.San Francisco, CA 94103. Retrieved from https://www.betterup.com/ blog/financial-stress.

Campbell, S. (2016). 6 Characteristics of resourceful people that bring them success. Retrieved from https://www.entrepreneur.com/article/272171.

Cassity,J. (n.d.) The benefits on looking at the bright side: 10n reasons to think like an optimist. Retrieved from https://www.happify.com/hd/10-reasons-to-think-like-an- optimist/.

CFI Team. (2021). Financial literacy. Retrieved from https://corporatefinanceinstitute .com/ resources/knowledge/finance/financial-literacy/

Ciperski, A. (2020). Creating plan to achieve data analytic success. Retrieved from https://www. qlik.com/blog/if-you-fail-to-plan-you-are-planning-to-fail-benjamin- franklin.

Chai,W. (2022). Continuous learning. WhatIs.com. Techtarget. Retrieved from https://www. techtarget.com/whatis/definition/continuous-learning.

Chatterjee,D. (2020). Why is it important to be optimistic in life and how to master it? Pinkvilla Desk. Retrieved from https://www.pinkvilla.com/lifestyle/people/why-it- important-stay-optimistic-life-and-how-master-it-570824.

Continuous Learning. (2022). Develop and maintain learning culture. Valamis. Retrieved from https://www.valamis.com/hub/continuous-learning.

Cote, C. (2020). The importance of financial literacy in business. Retrieved from https://online.hbs. edu/blog/post/importance-of-financial-literacy.

Coutinho, A. (2020). The power of positivity and openness. Retrieved from https://www.linkedin. com/pulse/power-positivity-openness-dr-alicia-coutinho.

Cronin, N. (2020). The different types of mentoring and how to use them. Retrieved from https:// www.guider-ai.com/blog/types-of-mentoring.

Cutler, Z. (2015). The 5 benefits of being optimistic. Retrieved from https://www. entrepreneur.com/ article/246204.

D'Angelo, M. (2022). How to find a mentor. Business news daily. Retrieved from https://www. businessnewsdaily.com/6248-how-to-find-mentor.html.

Del Mar, Z. (2021). Creating a school improvement plan that works. *Houghton Mifflin Harcourt.* Retrieved from https://www.hmhco.com/blog/creating-a-school- improvement-plan-that-works.

Dickerson, D. (2022). The power of resistance in leadership. Retrieved from https://www. dougdickerson.net/2022/05/08/the-power-of-resistance-in-leadership/

Fernando, J. (2022). Financial literacy definition. Investopedia. Retrieved from https://www. investopedia.com/terms/f/financial-literacy.asp.

Franken, J. (2020). How to be more receptive. Personality Profile Solutions, LLC 400 US-169 Suite #300 Minneapolis, MN. Retrieved from https://www.disc profiles.com/blog/2020/08/how-to-be-more-receptive/#.YyAfTHZBy3A.

Five Key Responsibilities- the school principal as a leader: guiding schools to better teaching and learning. (2021). Wallace. 140 Broadway, 49th Flr, New York, NY10005. Retrieved from https://www.wallacefoundation.org/knowledge- center/pages/key-responsibilities-the-school-principal-as-leader.aspx.

Goodyear, M. (2006). Mentoring: a learning collaboration. Retrieved from https://er.educause.edu/articles/2006/11/mentoring-a-learning-collaboration.

Hariharan, N.K., (2020). Rethinking budgeting in times of uncertainty. Sr. Hyperion SME & Department of Information Technology, United States. Retrieved from https://mpra.ub.uni-muenchen.de/109513/8/MPRA_paper_109513.pdf.

Head of School- Role and Responsibilities. (2013). Trinity College Dublin. The University of Dublin. College Green, Dublin 2, Ireland. Retrieved from https://www.tcd.ie/Secretary/academic-governance/head-of-school.php.

Hernando-Malipot, M. (2022). Capitalization threshold for school MOOE increased to 50,000. Manila Bulletin.Retrieved from https://mb.com.ph/2022/06/05/school- mooe-increased-to-p50k-deped/.

Horoszowski, M. (2020). How to build a great relationship with a mentor. Retrieved from https://hbr.org/2020/01/how-to-build-a-great-relationship-with-a-mentor

Indeed Editorial Team. (2022). What are resourcefulness skills? (And how to develop them). Indeed. Retrieved from https://au.indeed.com/career-advice/career- development/resourcefulness-skills.

Indeed Editorial Team. (2022). 23 Strategies to become more optimistic. Retrieved from https://www.indeed.com/career-advice/career-development/how-to-be-optimistic.

Jordan, K. (2020). Budgeting for uncertainty-the pandemic edition. MPI Financial and Insurance Planners Community Sponsor. Louisville. 1778. Retrieved from

https://www.mpi.org/blog/article/budgeting-for-uncertainty---the-pandemic-edition.

Karakus, M., Usak, M. & Ersozlu, A. (2018). Emotions in learning, teaching and leadership. A bibliometric review of Asian literature. SAGE journals. Retrieved from https://journals.sagepub.com/doi/10.1177/2158244020988865.

Kareem, O.A. & Kin, T.M. (2019). Emotional intelligence of school principals in managing change: Malaysian perspective. *Int. J. Management in Education.* (13). 3. Retrieved from https://www.researchgate.net/publication/334118515_ Emotional_intelligence_of_school_principals_in_ managing_change_Malaysian_p erspective.

Kim, J. (2020). Importance of optimism. Retrieved from https://edgearticles.com/ 2019/01/09/importance-of-optimism-essay/.

Kuligowski, K. (2022). 6 Leadership weaknesses and how to fix them. Retrieved from https://www. businessnewsdaily.com/7047-leadership-improvement.html

Lee, A. (2018). Be resourceful-one of the most important skills to succeed in data science. Retrieved from https://towardsdatascience.com/be-resourceful-one-of-the-most-important-skills-to-succeed-in-data-science-6ed5f33c2939

Lee, L. (2020). 7 Tips for effective school leadership. Administration and Leadership. Retrieved from https://www.edutopia.org/article/7-tips-effective-school-leadership.

Llego, M.A. (2019). DepEd releases revised guideline on schools MOOE. Retrieved from https:// www.teacherph.com/deped-revised-guidelines-on-schools-mooe/.

Lusardi, A. (2019). Financial literacy and the need for financial education: evidence and implication. Springer Open. Retrieved from https://sjes.springer open.com/ articles/10.1186/s41937-019-0027-5.

Macadatar, A. (2020). Six leadership qualities to improve school management. Retrieved from https://caraga.deped.gov.ph/six-leadership-qualities-to-improve-school-management/

Madison. (2019). 5 Steps to gain financial literacy. Retrieved from https://www. consumercredit. com/blog/5-steps-to-gain-financial-literacy/.

Maffea, J. (2020). Lack of resources in classrooms. Research Commons at Kutztown University. Retrieved from https://research.library.kutztown.edu/cgi/ viewcontent. cgi?article=1003&context=wickedproblems.

Maloney, D. (2020). The ultimate guide to remote working team collaboration. https://slack.com/ blog/collaboration/ultimate-guide-collaboration-in-the-workplace.

Mason, T.L. (2018). Emotionally connected: The role of emotional intelligence in the work of school leaders. Digital Commons at Georgia Southern. Georgia Southern University. Retrieved from https://digitalcommons.georgiasouthern.edu/ cgi/viewcontent. cgi?article=2876&context=etd.

Mautz, S. (2021). Issue #9: on the power of optimism, open-mindedness, and more. https://www. linkedin.com/pulse/issue-9-power-optimism-open-mindedness-more- scott-mautz/.

McGrath, M. (2018). Resourcefulness in the workplace: characteristics of a resourceful entrepreneur. Hiring & Empowering Solutions. Retrieved from https://hiringand empowering. com/resourcefulness-in-the-workplace-characteristics-of-a- resourceful-entrepreneur/.

McGurran, B. (2021). What is financial literacy and why is it important? Retrieved from https://www. experian.com/blogs/ask-experian/what-is-financial-literacy-and-why- is-it-important/.

Meador, D. (2019). The role of principals in schools. ThoughtCo. Retrieved from https://www. thoughtco.com/role-of-principal-in-schools-3194583.

Morin, A. (2022). Understanding trouble following directions. Retrieved from https://www.understood.org/en/articles/why-trouble-following-directions.

Morin, A. (2022). Being optimistic when the world around you isn't. Very well mind. Retrieved from https://www.verywellmind.com/how-to-be-optimistic-4164832.

Nathaniel, E.A. (2019). Impact of financial mismanagement among principals of Secondary schools in Benue State, Nigeria. Retrieved from https://www.researchgate.net/publication/338101356_IMPACT_OF_FINANCIAL_MISMANAGEMENT_AMONG_PRINCIPALS_OF_SECONDARY_SCHOOLS_IN_BENUE_STATE_NIGERIA

Nagpal, A. (2017). 7 Reasons why continuous learning is important. Retrieved from https://www.linkedin.com/pulse/7-reasons-why-continuous-learning-important- amit-nagpal/.

Neubauer, B.E. *et al*, (2019). How phenomenology can help us from the experiences of others? Retrieved from https://link.springer.com/article/10.1007/s40037-019- 0509-2.

Ochada, N. R, & Gempes, G. (2018). The realities of maintenance and operating expenses (mooe) allocation in basic education system: Unheard voices of public school teachers. International Journal of Scientific and Technology Research.

Retrieved from https://www.ijstr.org/final-print/apr2018/The-Realities-Of-Maintenance-And-Other-Operating-Expenses-mooe-Allocation-In-Basic-Education-System-Unheard-Voices-Of-Public-School-Teachers.pdf.

Ochieng, A. (2022) Why you should network with your peers, not just your mentors? Retrieved from https://sheleadsafrica.org/network-with-peers/.

Ordway, D.M. (2022). Being receptive to opposing views-why it matters (plus three tips for building rapport with distrustful sources). Retrieved from https://www. themandarin.com.au/179700-being-receptive-to-opposing-views-why-it-matters- plus-three-tips-for-building-rapport-with-distrustful-sources/.

Patrik, (2016). The key to meaningful productivity: Being receptive and (5 tips to make it happen). Buffer blog. Retrieved from https://buffer.com/resources/receptivity/.

Pattie, J. et al. (2018). Leading with emotional intelligence. ASCD. (77). 9. Retrieved from https://www.ascd.org/el/articles/leading-with-emotional-intelligence.

Peek, S. (2022). Peer mentoring is a mutually beneficial relationship that can advance your career. Business news daily. Retrieved from https://www.businessnewsdaily.com/7719-peer-mentoring.html.

Perestrelo, J.P. (2016). Mentoring of novice school principals by experienced principals in the Khomas region in Namibia. Retrieved from https://repository.unam.edu.na/bitstream/handle/11070/2046/perestrelo_2016.pdf?sequence=1&isAllowed=y

Principal job description: top duties and qualifications. (2022). Retrieved from https://www.indeed. com/recruitment/job-description/principal.

Renfro, 2021). 7 ways to manage financial stress during trying times. Bankrate, LLC. A Red Ventures company. Retrieved from https://www.bankrate.com/ banking/ways-to-manage-financial-stress/.

Rice,G. (2022). Continuous learning in the workplace. Thinkific Plus. Retrieved from https://www. thinkific.com/blog/continuous-learning/.

Robinson,L. & Smith,M. (2021). Coping with financial stress. Retrieved from https://www.helpguide. org/articles/stress/coping-with-financial-stress.htm.

Schooley, S. (2022). Career success depends on your willingness to learn. Retrieved from https:// www.businessnewsdaily.com/9256-career-boost-learning.html.

Scott, E. (2020). Wy is optimism? Verywellmind. Retrieved from https://www. verywellmind.com/ the-benefits-of-optimism-3144811.

Scott, E. (2022) Financial stress: how to cope. Verywellmind. Retrieved from https://www. verywellmind.com/understanding-and-preventing-financial-stress- 3144546.

Schwartz, K. (2018). How to plan continuous improvement in schools. KQED Mind Shift. Retrieved from   https://www.kqed.org/mindshift/51115/how-to-plan-and-implement-continuous-im-provement-in-schools.

Seven reasons why continuous learning is important. (2020). Education Executive. Retrieved from https://edexec.co.uk/seven-reasons-why-continuous-learning-is-important/.

Spacey, J. (2020). 9 Examples of mismanagement. Retrieved from https://simplicable.com/en/ mismanagement

Sriram. (2019). Top 10 issues around school management and how to solve them easily. Creatrix Campus. Retrieved from https://www.creatrixcampus.com/ blog/top-10-issues-around-school-management-and-how-solve-them-easily.

Stange, S. & Roos, A. (2020). Budgeting in an age uncertainty. Finance Function Excellence, Corporate Finance and Strategy, Strategic Planning. Retrieved from https://www.bcg.com/ publications/2020/budgeting-in-an-age-of-uncertainty.

Superville, D. (2019). For already burdened principals, budget control remains elusive. Education Week. https://www.edweek.org/leadership/for-already-burdened-principals-budget-control-remains-elusive/2019/09.

Sword, R. (2021). Why Is continuous learning important? Retrieved from https://www. highspeedtraining.co.uk/hub/why-is-continuous-learning-important/.

The Importance and Benefits of Continuous Learning. (2021). Tracom Group. 6675 South Kenton Street, Suite 118 Centennial, CO 80111. Retrieved from https://tracom.com/blog/the-importance-and-benefits-of-continuous-learning.

The importance of optimism to humanity in solving problems. (2020). Grades Fixer. Retrieved from https://gradesfixer.com/free-essay-examples/the-importance-of-optimism-to-humanity/.

The value of mentorship: collaboration is key to success. (2018). Prevue HR. Powered by Drive Digital. Retrieved from https://www.prevuehr.com/resources/insights/value-mentorship-collaboration-key-success/o.

Tina. (2022). The power of peer mentors at work. Retrieved from https://www. mentessa.com/posts/the-power-of-peer-mentors-at-work.

Tsuruo,S. (2020). The importance of mentorship, collaboration and slf-advocay. Office of undergraduate research. University of Connecticut. Retrieved from https://ugradresearch. uconn.edu/2020/11/12/the-importance-of-mentorship-collaboration-and-self-advocacy/#.

Udavant, S. (2020). How to be more receptive to learning opportunities as they come. Retrieved from https://medium.com/age-of-awareness/how-to-be-more-receptive-to-learning-opportunities-as-they-come-1fb1d10fd1f0.

Umoh, R. (2017). Why you should be highly optimistic if you want to be successful. Retrieved from https://www.cnbc.com/2017/10/05/why-should-you-be-highly-optimistic-if-you-want-to-be-successful.html.

Vogel, K. (n.d.). The 6 keys to effective collaboration in the workplace. Ring Central Blog. Retrieved from https://www.ringcentral.com/us/en/blog/collaboration-in-the-workplace/.

Yamamoto, J. et al. (2015). Emotion in leadership: secondary school administrator's perceptions of critical incidents. Education Management Administration & Leadership.https://www. researchgate.net/publication/273892037_Emotion_in_leadership_Secondary_school_ administrators%27_perceptions_of_critical_incidents

Webb, L. (2020). How to cope well with uncertainty. Retrieved from https://www.liggywebb.com/how-to-cope-well-with-uncertainty/

Witkin, G. (2019). 6 Ways to manage multiple emotions. Retrieved from https://www.psychologytoday. com/us/blog/the-chronicles-infertility/201904/6-ways-manage-multiple-emotions.

8020 Consulting Staff Writer. (2020). A look at budgeting and forecasting through uncertainty. Retrieved from https://8020consulting.com/budgeting-and-forecasting-uncertainty/.

ARCHIVAL LOG

MOOE PROCESS

(Follow Arrow)

PROCUREMENT PROCESS @ the School Level

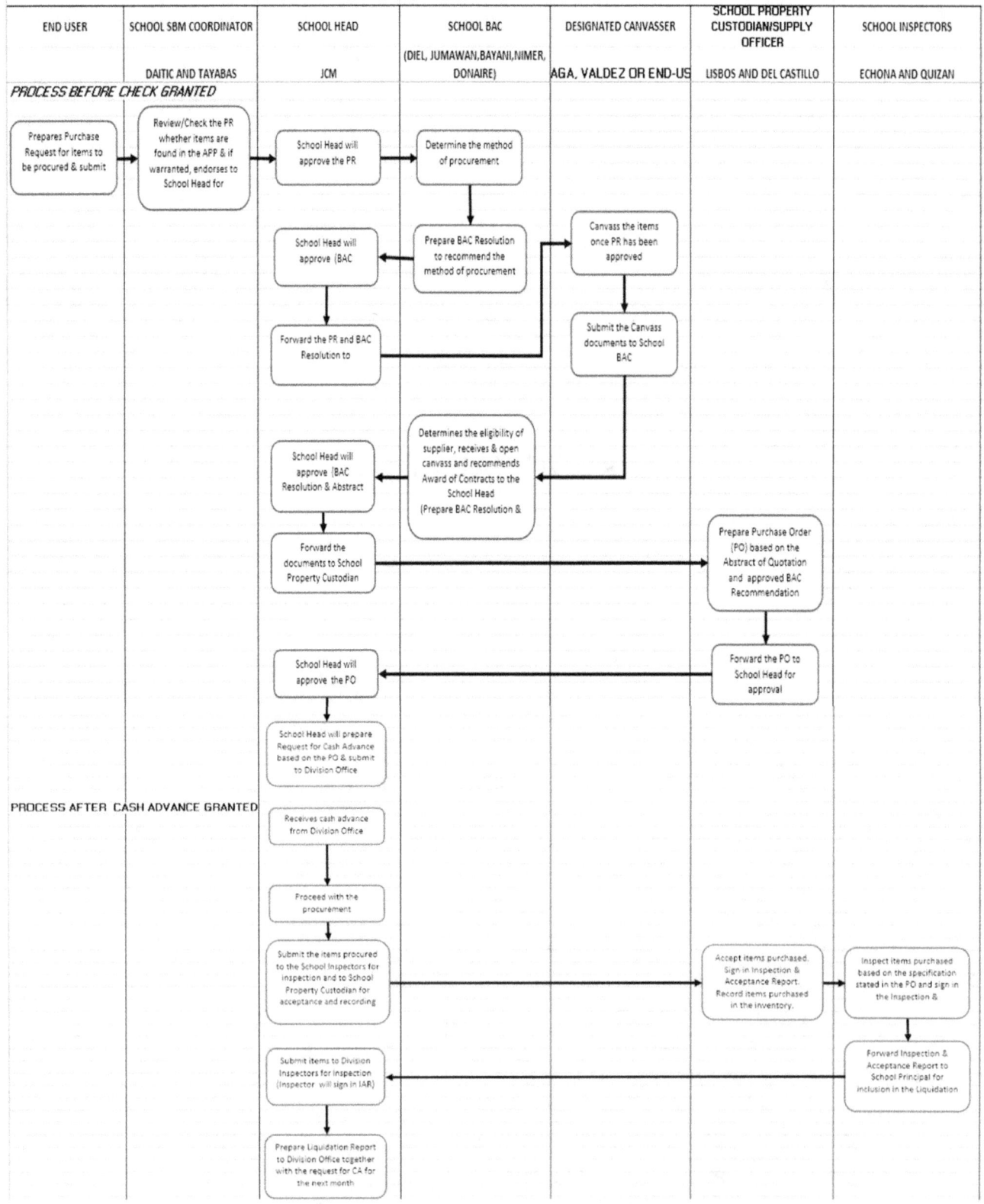

END USER	SCHOOL SBM COORDINATOR	SCHOOL HEAD	SCHOOL BAC	DESIGNATED CANVASSER	SCHOOL PROPERTY CUSTODIAN/SUPPLY OFFICER	SCHOOL INSPECTORS
			(DIEL, JUMAWAN,BAYANI,NIMER, DONAIRE)			
	DAITIC AND TAYABAS	JCM		AGA, VALDEZ OR END-US	LISBOS AND DEL CASTILLO	ECHONA AND QUIZAN

PROCESS BEFORE CHECK GRANTED

- Prepares Purchase Request for items to be procured & submit
- Review/Check the PR whether items are found in the APP & if warranted, endorses to School Head for
- School Head will approve the PR
- Determine the method of procurement
- School Head will approve (BAC
- Prepare BAC Resolution to recommend the method of procurement
- Canvass the items once PR has been approved
- Forward the PR and BAC Resolution to
- Submit the Canvass documents to School BAC
- Determines the eligibility of supplier, receives & open canvass and recommends Award of Contracts to the School Head (Prepare BAC Resolution &
- School Head will approve (BAC Resolution & Abstract
- Forward the documents to School Property Custodian
- Prepare Purchase Order (PO) based on the Abstract of Quotation and approved BAC Recommendation
- Forward the PO to School Head for approval
- School Head will approve the PO
- School Head will prepare Request for Cash Advance based on the PO & submit to Division Office

PROCESS AFTER CASH ADVANCE GRANTED

- Receives cash advance from Division Office
- Proceed with the procurement
- Submit the items procured to the School Inspectors for inspection and to School Property Custodian for acceptance and recording
- Accept items purchased. Sign in Inspection & Acceptance Report. Record items purchased in the inventory.
- Inspect items purchased based on the specification stated in the PO and sign in the Inspection &
- Submit items to Division Inspectors for inspection (Inspector will sign in IAR)
- Forward Inspection & Acceptance Report to School Principal for inclusion in the Liquidation
- Prepare Liquidation Report to Division Office together with the request for CA for the next month

UMERC CERTIFICATE

ETHICS REVIEW COMMITTEE (UMERC)
Ground Floor, Professional Schools Building
Ma-a Matina Campus, Davao City
Telephone: (082)305-0640 local 189
umethicsreviewer@umindanao.edu.ph

FORM 2.6
Certificate of Approval

Date   May 30, 2022

This is to certify that the following protocol and related documents have been granted approval by the **University of Mindanao Ethics Review Committee** for implementation.

UMERC Protocol No.	UMERC-2022-172	Sponsor Protocol No	N/A
Principal Investigator/s	JULIE ANN D. BAYANI	Sponsor	N/A
Title	Travails of Novice Principals as Fiscal Managers		
Protocol Version No.	2	Version Date	May 28, 2022
ICF Version No. Other documents	1	Version Date	March 10, 2022
Members of research team Study sites	Davao Region		

Type of review	☑ Expedited ☐ Full board	**Duration of Approval:** May 28, 2022 – November 28, 2022	**Approved Meeting Date:** May 28, 2022

UMERC Chairperson	Signature	Date	
HELEN Q. OMBLERO, DSD		May 28, 2022	

ETHICS REVIEW COMMITTEE (UMERC)
Ground Floor, Professional Schools Building
Ma-a Matina Campus, Davao City
Telephone: (082)305-0640 local 189
umethicsreviewer@umindanao.edu.ph

Received by:

Name   JULIE ANN D. BAYANI

Signature   Date   May 30, 2022

The University of Mindanao

CERTIFICATE

OF APPRECIATION

is given to

JULIE ANN D. BAYANI

as *RESOURCE SPEAKER*

during the Online Public Research Forum with the theme
"Inspiring Change and Innovation in Education: A Research Forum"

Given this 1st day of July 2022 at the
Professional Schools, University of Mindanao, Davao City

JOEL B. TAN. DBA
Research Coornidator

SITTI ROGAIYA L. APADAN, RSW
AVP, Community Extension
& Outreach

EUGENIO S. GUHAO, JR., DM
Dean

QUESTIONNAIRE VALIDATION SHEET

	PROFESSIONAL SCHOOLS
	[/] Main [ ] Branch _____
	VALIDATION SHEET FOR RESEARCH QUESTIONNAIRE - QUALITATIVE

The University of Mindanao

Name of Evaluator : Joel B. Tan

Degree : CPA/DBA

Position : Research Coordinator

To the Evaluator : Kindly check column which fits your evaluation for the item.

RATING: Number of YES marks

[ ] 10 Very Good   [ ] 6-7 May be upgraded if revised

[/] 8-9 Good   [ ] 0-5 For revalidation

ITEMS	YES	NO
Ethics		
1. Introduction (purpose, confidentiality, duration and way of conduct and closing components for additional comments) are provided.		/
2. Informed consent is included.		/
Artistry		
3. Script is included/built in, so interview can introduce, guide and conclude the interview in a consistent manner.	/	
4. Questions are appropriate to the study enhancing the possibility of storytelling and narratives.	/	
Rigor		
5. Questions are open-ended to encourage in depth responses; avoiding close-ended questions which are answered by "Yes" or "No".	/	
6. Questions are stated in the affirmative.	/	
7. Probe questions are provided.	/	
8. Questions are logically ordered asking the highest priority first. Opinion questions follow information questions.	/	
9. Questions are stated in clear and simple terms.	/	
10. Number of questions can be covered within 60-90 minutes, not exceeding 15 open-ended items (probes excluded) for every research questions, except special cases.	/	

Title of Approved Research : Travails of Novice Principals as Fiscal Managers

Name of Researcher : **JULIE ANN D. BAYANI**

Degree Enrolled : MAED - EM

Research Adviser : EUNICE A. ATIENZAR, PhD

Date of Evaluation of Questionnaire: **August 11, 2020**

Remarks of the Evaluator : Please see comments. Revise your instrument as suggested before administration

Joel B. Tan

Signature of Evaluator above Printed Name

PROFESSIONAL SCHOOLS

[⨯] Main   [   ] Branch _____

VALIDATION SHEET FOR RESEARCH QUESTIONNAIRE - QUALITATIVE

Name of Evaluator   :   LYNDON A. QUINES

Degree   :   DOCTOR OF EDUCATION

Position   :   PROFESSOR

To the Evaluator   : Kindly check column which fits your evaluation for the item.

RATING: Number of YES marks

[   ] 10 Very Good   [ ] 6-7 May be upgraded if revised

[   ] 8-9 Good   [ ] 0-5 For revalidation

ITEMS	YES	NO
Ethics		
1. Introduction (purpose, confidentiality, duration and way of conduct and closing components for additional comments) are provided.	✓	
2. Informed consent is included.	✓	
Artistry		
3. Script is included/built in, so interview can introduce, guide and conclude the interview in a consistent manner.	✓	
4. Questions are appropriate to the study enhancing the possibility of storytelling and narratives.	✓	
Rigor		
5. Questions are open-ended to encourage in depth responses; avoiding close-ended questions which are answered by "Yes" or "No".	✓	
6. Questions are stated in the affirmative.	✓	
7. Probe questions are provided.	✓	
8. Questions are logically ordered asking the highest priority first. Opinion questions follow information questions.	✓	
9. Questions are stated in clear and simple terms.	✓	
10. Number of questions can be covered within 60-90 minutes, not exceeding 15 open-ended items (probes excluded) for every research questions, except special cases.	✓	

Title of Approved Research   : Travails of Novice Principals as Fiscal Managers

Name of Researcher   : Julie Ann D. Bayani

Degree Enrolled   : Master of Education Major in Educational Management

Research Adviser   : Dr. Eunice A. Atienzar

Date of Evaluation of Questionnaire: 3/16/2022

Remarks of the Evaluator   :   Follow suggestions/recommendations

LYNDON A. QUINES, EdD

Signature of Evaluator Above Printed Name

PROFESSIONAL SCHOOLS

[⨼] Main [ ] Branch _____

VALIDATION SHEET FOR RESEARCH QUESTIONNAIRE - QUALITATIVE

Name of Evaluator : Rinante L. Genuba, EdD

Degree : Doctor of Education

Position : Prof II

To the Evaluator : Kindly check column which fits your evaluation for the item.

RATING: Number of YES marks

[ ] 10 Very Good   [ ] 6-7 May be upgraded if revised

[ ] 8-9 Good   [ ] 0-5 For revalidation

ITEMS	YES	NO
Ethics		
1. Introduction (purpose, confidentiality, duration and way of conduct and closing components for additional comments) are provided.	/	
2. Informed consent is included.		
Artistry		
3. Script is included/built in, so interview can introduce, guide and conclude the interview in a consistent manner.	/	
4. Questions are appropriate to the study enhancing the possibility of storytelling and narratives.	/	
Rigor		
5. Questions are open-ended to encourage in depth responses; avoiding close-ended questions which are answered by "Yes" or "No".	/	
6. Questions are stated in the affirmative.	/	
7. Probe questions are provided.		
8. Questions are logically ordered asking the highest priority first. Opinion questions follow information questions.	/	
9. Questions are stated in clear and simple terms.	/	
10. Number of questions can be covered within 60-90 minutes, not exceeding 15 open-ended items (probes excluded) for every research questions, except special cases.	/	

Title of Approved Research : Travails of Novice Principals as Fiscal Managers

Name of Researcher : Julie Ann D. Bayani

Degree Enrolled : Master of Education Major in Educational Management

Research Adviser : Dr. Eunice A. Atienzar

Date of Evaluation of Questionnaire: March 12, 2022

Remarks of the Evaluator : Ok for administration

RINANTE L. GENUBA, EdD
Signature of Evaluator Above Printed Name

F-13580-031/ Rev. #0/ Effectivity: February 1, 2019

PROFESSIONAL SCHOOLS

[_] Main [ ] Branch _____

VALIDATION SHEET FOR RESEARCH QUESTIONNAIRE - QUALITATIVE

Name of Evaluator : Dr. Bacasmot

Degree : PhD

Position : PC

To the Evaluator : Kindly check column which fits your evaluation for the item.

RATING: Number of YES marks

[_] 10 Very Good   [ ] 6-7 May be upgraded if revised
[_] 8-9 Good   [ ] 0-5 For revalidation

ITEMS	YES	NO
Ethics		
1. Introduction (purpose, confidentiality, duration and way of conduct and closing components for additional comments) are provided.		/
2. Informed consent is included.		/
Artistry		
3. Script is included/built in, so interview can introduce, guide and conclude the interview in a consistent manner.		/
4. Questions are appropriate to the study enhancing the possibility of storytelling and narratives.	/	
Rigor		
5. Questions are open-ended to encourage in depth responses; avoiding close-ended questions which are answered by "Yes" or "No".	/	
6. Questions are stated in the affirmative.	/	
7. Probe questions are provided.		
8. Questions are logically ordered asking the highest priority first. Opinion questions follow information questions.	/	
9. Questions are stated in clear and simple terms.	/	
10. Number of questions can be covered within 60-90 minutes, not exceeding 15 open-ended items (probes excluded) for every research questions, except special cases.	/	

Title of Approved Research _: Travails of Novice Principals as Fiscal Managers
_____

Name of Researcher : Julie Ann D. Bayani

Degree Enrolled : Master of Education Major in Educational Management

Research Adviser : Dr. Eunice A. Atienzar

Date of Evaluation of Questionnaire: March 13, 2022

Remarks of the Evaluator : Please include what are lacking; improve the research tool; the format is confusing; I suggest you present in matrix form.

Dr. JOCLEYN B. BACASMOT
_____
Signature of Evaluator Above Printed Name

INFORMED CONSENT FORM

University of Mindanao

Informed Consent Form (ICF)

UMERC - 006
Rev. 01 / December 1, 2016
Approved by:

Control No.:

University of Mindanao Ethics Review Committee
Matina, Davao City

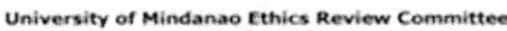

Informed Consent Form for (Travails of Novice Principals as Fiscal Managers)
Name of the Researcher(s) Julie Ann D. Bayani
Institution: University of Mindanao

INTRODUCTION

You are invited to participate in a research study conducted by Julie Ann D. Bayani, at the University of Mindanao, because you fit the inclusion criteria for informants of our study.

Your participation is completely voluntary. Please read the information below, and ask questions about anything you do not understand, before deciding whether to participate. Please take as much time as you need to read the consent form. You may also decide to discuss participation with your family or friends.

If you decide to participate, you will be asked to sign this form. You will be given a copy of this form.

PURPOSE OF THE STUDY
This study aims to predict the set of guidelines for the aspiring future school heads or principals in handling school finances.

STUDY PROCEDURES
If you volunteer to participate in this study, you will be asked to participate by answering the survey questionnaire which you can finish in less than 30 minutes.

POTENTIAL RISKS AND DISCOMFORTS
You may feel discomfort during the course of the interview because of the sensitive nature of the topic being studied. You may opt not to answer questions which make you feel any psychological or emotional distress or you can withdraw as a participant of the study if you feel that you cannot discuss the information that is asked of you. The researchers value your participation and will place your welfare as their highest priority during the course of the study.

POTENTIAL BENEFITS TO PARTICIPANTS AND/OR TO SOCIETY
This study can generate relevant information which can be useful to public and private administrators, human resource managers, and policy-makers. The results, discussions, and findings from this study can spark evidence-based information which can be used by government agencies such as Department of Education.

CONFIDENTIALITY
We will keep your records for this study confidential as far as permitted by law. Any identifiable information obtained in connection with this study will remain confidential, except if necessary to protect your rights or welfare. This certificate means that the researcher can resist the release of information about your participation to people who are not connected with the study. When the results of the research are published or discussed in conferences, no identifiable information will be used.

INVESTIGATOR'S CONTACT INFORMATION
If you have any questions or concerns about the research, please feel free to contact the researcher at the Deca Homes, Tigatto, Davao City through telephone number 221 or mobile phone number 09514551847 or through email at bayanijulieann11@gmail.com; or if you need to see her, she can be located at the Office of the Communal NHS, Davao City.

RIGHTS OF RESEARCH PARTICIPANT
If you have questions, concerns, or complaints about your right as a research participant or the research in general and are unable to contact the research team, or if you want to talk to someone independent of the research team, please contact the University of Mindanao Professional Schools at 305-06-45

RESEARCH PARTICIPANT'S CONSENT

I have read the information provided above. I have been given a chance to ask questions. My questions have been answered to my satisfaction, and I agree to participate in this study. I have been given a copy of this form. I can withdraw my consent at any time and discontinue participation without penalty.

_____   **March 10, 2022**
Signature above Printed Name of Participant   **Date Signed**

To be accomplished by the Researcher Obtaining Consent:
I have explained the research to the participant and answered all of his/her questions. I believe that he/she understands the information described in this document and freely consents to participate.

_____   **March 10, 2022**
JULIE ANN D. BAYANI   **Date Signed**
Name of Person Obtaining Consent

Research Questionnaire

"Travails of Novice Principals as Fiscal Managers"

Name:
Position:
Years in the Service:
School:
Contact Number:
Email address:

1. What are the experiences of novice principals as fiscal managers?

Guide Questions:

a. How do you feel during your primary years in handling school fund?

b. Recently, several schools were mentioned due to unobligated amount of their MOOE for fiscal year 2021. How do you manage your time in handling school finances so that this kind of incidence will be avoided?

c. Being a novice school head, how do you find the guidelines and system that were being implemented by the central office and division office with regards to MOOE?

d. What are the factors that you need to consider in handling school finances?

e. When it becomes to school needs, differentiate your level of concerns now that you are the school head compared when you were once a teacher?

Probe Questions:

1. What are some difficulties you find in following the MOOE guidelines?

2. Was there a time that you thought of giving up from the job?

2. How do they cope with the challenges or obstacles as fiscal managers?

a. Who are the people that has been helping you function well as fiscal manager? What kind of help they have already extended to you in this matter?

b. What are the learning programs that really equip you in handling school resources?

c. As to what extent were you able to explore in addressing school concerns?

d. There are times that the requested monthly/quarterly MOOE are delayed and you have a so many needs in that specific time. How were you able to compose yourself and remain optimistic in this kind of situation?

e. What are best your best practices as to overcoming the obstacles of being the school fund manager?

Probe Questions:

1. How do you manage your time well considering the fact that being a school head equates various jobs?

2. Why do you think there is a need to always connect to your mentors and colleagues in this field?

3. What are the insights that can be drawn from this study?

Guide Questions:

a. As school head, how do you establish your authority as fiscal manger?

b. Being new in the job, how important it is for you to connect with the peers and mentors in the field to be able to gain more knowledge on this certain task?

c. How significant it is for you to be literate in fiscal management?

d. Why do you think you need to be transparent as fiscal manager?

e. How essential it is to possess positive and good attitude as a school leader particularly in handling school resources?

Probe Questions?

1. How do you deal with oppositions when it comes to budgeting?

2. In what way, you are able to manifest your optimism with regards to financial management?

IN-DEPTH INTERVIEW GUIDE QUESTIONS

Research Questionnaire

Title: "Travails of Novice Principals as Fiscal Managers"

Name:
Position:
Years in the Service:
School:
Contact Number:
Email address:

1. What are the experiences of novice principals as fiscal managers?

    a. What are the negative emotions that creep in during your primary years in the job?

    b. Do you struggle with time constraints? Why?

    c. Being the novice school head, how do you find the curriculum and policies at this level?

    d. What are the things that you need to consider in handling school finances?

    e. Differentiate the obstacles now that you are the school head from being a teacher before?

2. How do they cope with the challenges or obstacles as fiscal managers?

    a. How does your colleagues and mentors help you in this new position?

    b. What are the learning programs that really help you in this job?

    c. Being resourceful is one of the attitudes you need to possess in this job, to what extent were you able to explore in addressing school concerns?

    d. In the midst of setbacks, how are you able to manifest optimism in every situation?

3. What are the insights that can be drawn from this study?

    a. As school head, how do you establish your authority?

    b. Being new in the job, how important it is for you to connect with the peers and mentors in the field?

    c. How significant it is for you to be literate in fiscal management?

    d. Why do you think you need to have a receptive character in this new position?

    e. How essential it is to possess positive and good attitude as a school leader?

FOCUS GROUP DISCUSSION PICTURES

AND LINKS FOR RECORDINGS

Recording links: https://drive.google.com/file/d/11Bog1_crp030oa-gj7rTxTCEOYS6QFfx/ view

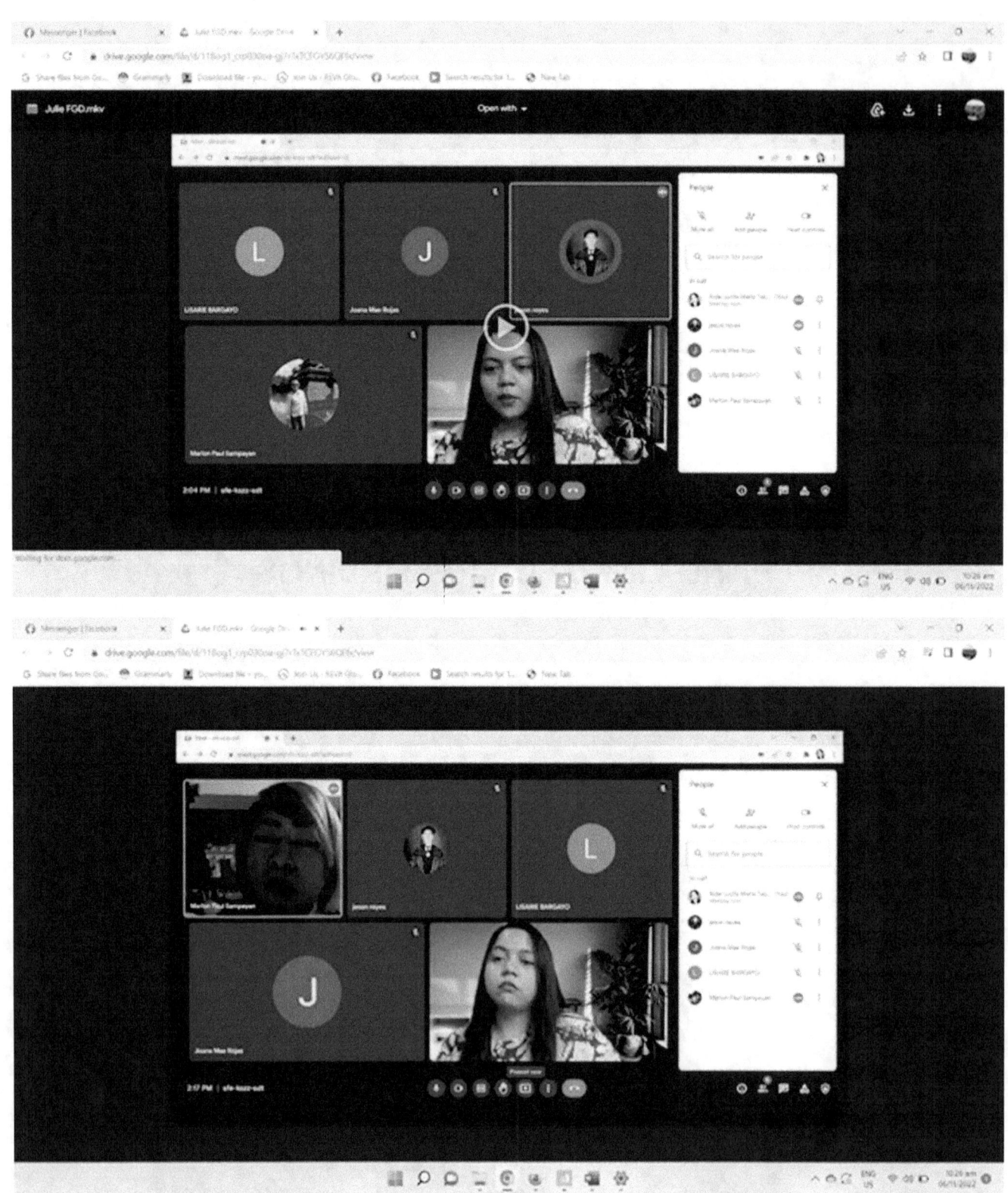

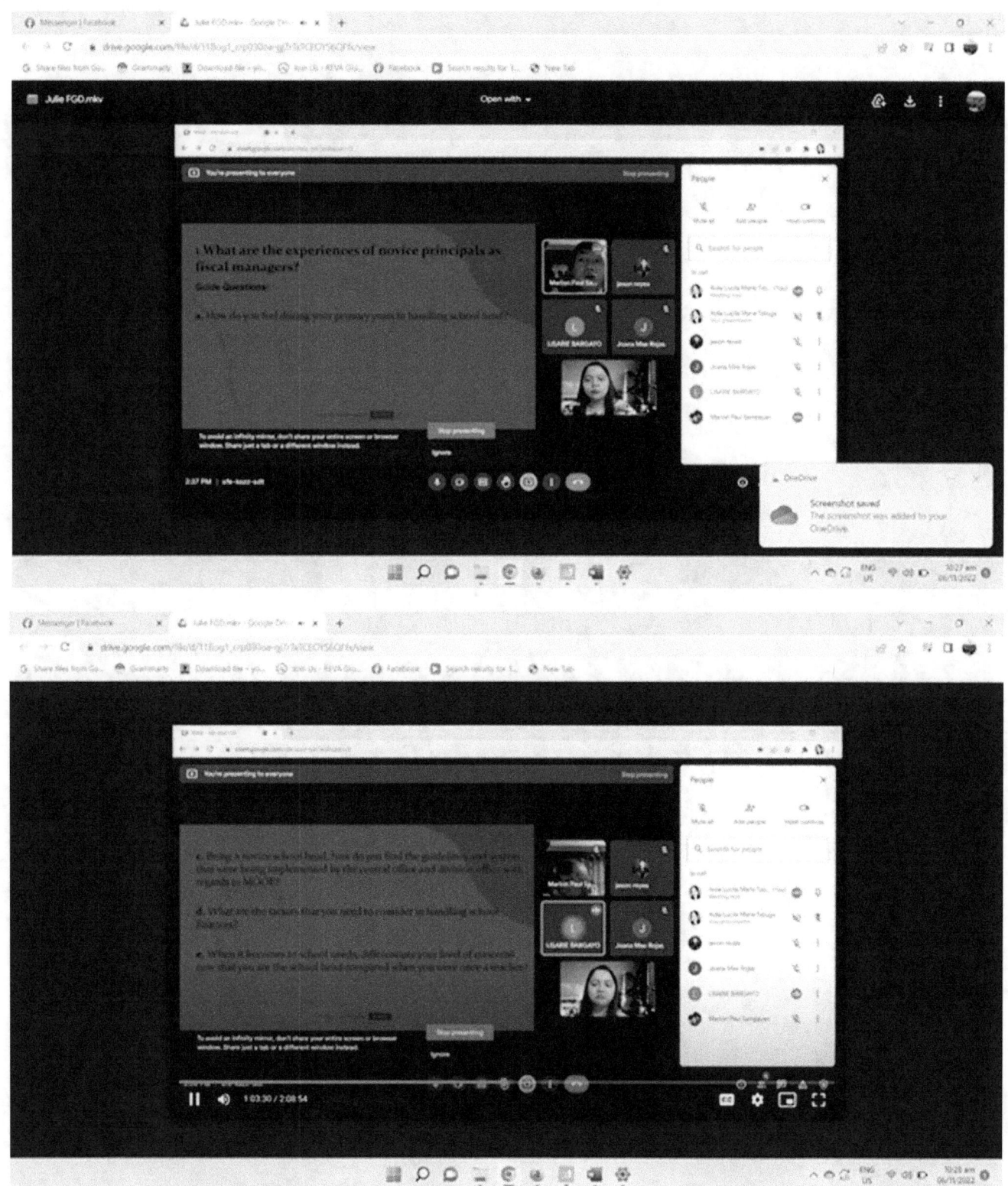

TRANSCRIPTION ON FOCUS GROUP DISCUSSION

TRAVAILS OF NOVICE PRINCIPAL AS FISCALS MANAGEMENT

1. What are the experiences if the novice principal as fiscal managers?

a. How do you feel during your primary years in handling school funds? 17:40

- JOANA MAE ROJAS:

  So how do I feel during my primary years kanang grabe jud nakahilak jud ko aning MOOE kaning school fund luckily ahh kanang blessed ra pud ko kay under me sa isa ka cluster no tulo me ka school together with Lumad Elementary School so gi assist pud ko niya nga dili me ma behind kay big deal man pud kaau baya ang liquidation sa school fund nya ako aminado jud ko na weakness jdu nako na kay dili ko ganahan mag sigeg kanang compute kanang mga BIR forms karon kanang mag dili gyud kay weakness jud na nako so I really felt kanang makulbaan ko ma pressure ko kay syempre kwarta baya na sa skwelahan so mao to jul.

- LISARIE BARGAYO

  Am wala kaau nako na feel na kay tungod una wala man gud koy MOOE nga iliquidate ang pag start gyud amm while I understand ah na lisod gyud ang kahimtang before ko niad2 naa na sa akoang hunahuna nga lisod gyud ang kahimtang because I also started tugbok national high school before I am one of the pioneer teachers and maka I mean naagian na nako ang experience so murag medjo taas ang akong patience with it come to kalisod sa school especially sa fund ang thingking lang nako that time pag start sa skwelahan is for as long as mahatag ang basic needs sa school okay rako I can sustain for siguro years ana and so ang basic lang man gyud nako that time is kanang teacher, kinahangkan ko teacher and room since naa me sa elementary so dili wala kaau ko nag problema tapos gamay lang pud ang among studyante ingonana but then came na ang mother school pud namo kanang tight n apud ilahang funds so medyo lisod lisod na gyud ni sya nagka lisod lisod na I mean naa na koy mga request na dili na sya mahatag so on and so forth. But learnings still continue kay am luckily nagkaroon pud ko in just a year nagkaroon ko ug 4 teachers pagsugod nako so dili kayo sya bug.at kay mo go on lang man gyud ang klase maski ugbwala pa ghyud me kwarta kay naa amay teachers but then ahm karon nag transfer na me ug bag.ong capus diri ang kalisod na kuan nako ang kalisod pero ang ang ang ang back nako ang kanang bang murag ang atrasan alng gyud nako is for as long as naa koy teacher mo go on ra jud ang klase mao ra gyud na akoa so naa lay mga ah kaning need lang gyud pareho karon na kanang mga modules kana murag medyo nalisuran me kay ang fund pud namo ang PTA fund wala pud kaau me kuan ing.ana pero am sa mga pinaka impoertante na mag need sa school naga rely ra lang gyud ko sa PTA . so to kaning para mag karoon kog fund lang gyud na magamit sa school kasi gina plano man gyud na nato to ahead no na na mao ni ang mga need sa school so kinanghanglan na pangitaan nato syag fund so at at a kaning the start of the school year naka plano na naka implement nako kung unsaon pag collect ang fund biski dili pa sya kinahangan ang sa akoa is dapat ma collect na sya kay in times na need na gyud kaau kung wala na juy kwarta naan na tay pundo kay it will take ma jud time to kaning collect no mga fund na ingon ani na dili gikan s gobyerno. Now when it comes to kaning am kaning experience of kaning ehem kaning technichalites sa kaning MOOE kaning liquidation kanang ingon ana am I have I had an experience pud in 2010 kadtong under pa pud me sa mintal comprehensive international high school am implementing unit ang compre so ah naa me alote na tagaan me kwarta gikan sa compre kami na ang mag process sa liquidation since ang implementing unit is naa gyud na silay ilahang coa ang standard nila is different from the division office when it come to liquidation that time 2010 and am that time pud I was trained ah sa kaning liquidation sa mga unsa panang mga trabaho dinha by kaning an adas ng compre na nag serve na sya taas taas nga times sa USEP mintal which is a national pud ang iyahang take university which is mas mas mas kaning komplikado ang ilahang system no so when it comes to details unsaon pag liquidate and all makahilak hilak gyud ko that time kay kana bang teacher ra man ko nya kanang wala lang jud laing nasugo baa ko ra juy na-sugoan nya sayun lang sya buhaton kay prepared naman ang mga forms pero pag mamali kag singko sintabos ana gani naa kay mamali gamay di pweding irson nya human I feel na kanang strikta ra jud kaau ang ADAS ato na time lami na gyud kaau buhian ang trabaho gani kanang Hoi ginoo ko mao ra jud ni akong hilakan wala man gani ko naghilak hilak sa akong pag panudlo kani lang jud hinuon na dili pa jud nako kanang I mean ing.ana ba so pero giagwanta nako lang jdu to nako sya hangtod niabot ang time na nakakita ko ug pamaagi na makahawa ko ani na trabaho and I would say na dili sya maau nga exit nako that time kay napuno na gyud ko aning trabhua AHAHA not knowing nga amo ra diay gihapon ang akong subayon pero karon because that time oo vbecause that time wala man gyud ko naghuna-huna gyud na mag school head you know na pagka novice ka ka sa teaching pagsugod pa lang nimo earlier nimo until ano to 5-10 years dili paka makahuna huna na I do not know no dili man gyud pareho ang teacher gyud pud but that tiem wala gyud koy huna huna nga ang akong gi huna huna nga ma promote kos iguro pinaka taas na maka master teacher ko but I was working on that una hatagan ko nya wala na hinoon ko advisory kay kinahanglan na tanggalan ko advisory kay magtaniman ko sa kwarta ana ba murag mag huna huna ko na unsa naman ni oi dili man ko gusto ani nga trabaho ana ba and I mga siguro mga 10 years pud ko nga walay advisory that time kay tabok tabok akong trabaho from property custodian to kaning MOOE at hangtod na ako nay property custodian as the same time ako pay MOOE nakaingon ko sa akong principal na Sir mapurdoy gyud ka aning imohang kala-ki madaghan ma dato ko ani. Sya ngano man? Ana ko na pwede ra gud akoy maghimo sa inventory akoy mu liquidate akoy mupalit akoy muhimo ug kanang request naunsa nya ikaw ra ba sir di baya ka kabalo ug asa nako gipamutagng mga gipamunit nato mga diba mga ingon ana. Ingon ko for delikadisa sir pangita ug lain nga akong tagaan ug kaning property custodian kay though I know ingon sya na dai wala koy lain ma trust na saligan sa trabaho ikaw lang ingon ko yes sir kasabot ko ana pero dili pud pwede pud na tirahon ko musugot ra kang tira tirahon ko miski wala ko kay gihimo diri mga ingon ana. So pagka karon kay Naki-ta nako na ang process ng division sa mga non implementing unit is almost the same sa akong naagian atong 2010. So I;ve said nga kung ingon ani lang siguro kung lang gyud kaau ko makaya kaya pa I mean ive been liquidating MOOE for three years ata to na time bago ko ni exit gyud and siguro ang kalisod lang man sa MOOE I mean sa atoa I mean sa amoa nga school head about ning fiscal kaning ilahang terms di man gud ko kasabot anang diba mga accounting terms ba nga unsa diay na ay mao ra man diay ni pasabot ani murag ana ba. So murag familiar na ang mga terms gamay pero mas murag tan.aw nako mas mag level up pa ata ang skill na kinahanglan nako as school head na karon as a school head because its different before pwede rako mag liquidate ug nay sayop kay unsa mani sir na late okay rana si sir bitaw pang tawagon di bitaw ako murag something ana but now as a school head the responsibility and the accountaility to make it on time sa ako na jud sya padulong mao na sya pero as of karon funding sa school lisod gyud sya lisod kaau mangita. Unfortunately, sugod pag sugod wala gyud me alote form our mother school so same with sir marlon it was only last January nga I wrote a letter to the SDS and the PSDS actually ay no I wrote a letter to the principal ng mother school copyfurnish sa SDS at sa PSDS requesting an alotement alote lang gyud bahalag di me tagaan kwarta basta tagaan meg alote nga kani inyong kwarta pwede mo mag request atleast ang akoang ma request is amoang concerns sa school because they are request man gud nako karon nga nay mother school mupalit man sila pero usahay tungod wala sa ialahang APPT kay established na man gud sila kami dili pa so different ang among need sa ilahang need ang priority namo kay bondpaper ila di mana nila kau nila priority ang bondpaper kay online naa man silay online mga ingon ana ba. So given nga matagaan gihapon ko pero dili pud sya, gawas na limited maam dili pa jud sya ang need kaau nako murag ana ba kanang naam aga. Kay ngano man mao lang pud ang naa sa ilahang ATp. We cannot make our own project for example kang physical kanag learning environment mag lisod kog request ug hallowblock ug semento kay dili man sila musalig sa amoa nga kaya namo iliquidate na or madungagan man ang ilahang trabaho to liquidate and purchase materials kay diba iad2 pa gud nila sa among skwela nya sila kay ana ba so I understand also the situation of the mother school mao na sya nga ang akong gipangayo sa ilaha just give us an alotement so we can align our kaning request sa direction ng school namo as a newly established school mga ingon ana. Though I know nan aa gihapon nay limitasyon tungod kay it will depend in the ATP of the mother school kay ilaha mang kwarta sila may mag liquidate so did2 gihapon ko mutan.aw sa ilahang ATP pero at least kana bang kaya ra nako syang I himooan ug pamaagi nga kani wa gyud me ani nag request pero mao ni naa sa ilahang ATP ah kani ang among pwede mahimo ani nga mga butang something ingon ana ba kaya ra kayaa ra nako sya planohan mga ana.

- JESON REYES

Nor regarding with the question no I want to state that the my experience handling the school fund is somewhat mix emotion in a sense that I am quite happy that because I have school fund however in terms of managing it in terms of the school projects it will be mix emotions to me since I am a newly hired school head so that is somewhat mis emotion lang maam jul, maybe later I could share a lot of experiences depending on the questions but as of the moment I could say that my feeling now is somewhat mix emotions especially handling school fund ive experience to have PTA collections since I started a school in a year 2020 and I also have MOOE in the same year so both ive experience PTA nad MOOE and from that sense I can say that I happy yet sad sometimes shock with the rules and regulations in the department of education thank you and good afternoon.

- MARLON PAUL

Actually theres a lot of definition about school funds because you can also get it from link-ages so there are people there are sponsoring agencies that will give you fund, money or in kind, as to that I don't have any problem about that because I when I accepeted donation I eventually or not eventually I directly purchased the money or the items and then I need to gave them proof just to make them feel na I am being honest as the school head were being honest as a school kasi naa koy mga lingkages na they will send me in my person-al account actually but because I theres a lot of materials or theres a lot of things that we needed in school and I have some lingkages abroad also here in davao city they are9 willing to give you support. In terms of handling I don't have any problem because I am very trans-parent with my teacgers even to awards because our school is recently received an award with a reward no naa syay gift cards an amount of 7,000 so I told the teachers na what to purchase and what is my priority for that amount so part of the school fund parin so I am so being transparent. no problem at all, there are speculations maybe in their mind na unsa ba . pero I am very transparent kasi nakikita naman sa school na binigay ko talaga, as to kanang fiscal mamangement wala na koy problem ana ang kana mang gung allocation for us appropriation for the mother sxhool dili na lang ko nagahuna huna gud ingon ana ilaha nalang to though ang amoa man gung learners naka encode sa ilahang school ID so nay appropriate nay equivalent every learner every teacher every class room so naa tay kuan ana tung fiscal. Parang nay computation man gud every learner every teacher every kuan so wla naman na hatag so okay ra way problema. Problema gud sya gud pero kuan ba plastic lang ko ba na kaya nako. You nee to be kuan man gud you need to find ways gud no kanang ikaw man gud ang leader so ikaw ang mangita paraan though we have to dol out we have to shell out from your own pocket just to sustain their needs sa teachers kay naa puy mga teachers nan aa pud silay sariling pangangailangan man gud so you cannot kay loy pud kaau they have their own kanang mga kuan sa ilang balay breadwinner sila kanang ang pag adto pa jud sa skwelahan kay very far so kailangan ug kanang kwarta so dili nimo mapugos tanan na ipaamot sa ilaha tanan. Pero equally divided jud jud me ako tung una ako gyud tanan. Karon pud ako tanan kay magbisita man gud akoang mga school head puhon march 11. So walay laing kuan ako. Nya lisod man pug magpaamot kas community kay hasta pud nilang lisura . so maski pag PTA funds hurot. Diba naa man ta GSP na kana kailangan nato iregister even kanang GAT a kanang sponsor sa GSP registration . so walay problema ang parents kay nakapangita mna kog ug sponsor sa GSP registration na which is 2700 apil pa jud ang parents I register. So wala nay problema ang parents ako nay ni shoulder ato from the sponsors man.

b. Recently, several schools were mentioned due to unobligated amount of their MOOE for fiscal year 2021. How do you manage your time in handling school finances so that this kind of incidence will be avoided? **36:51**

- JESON REYES

Regarding with your question no sa unobligated my school is one of the list school in unobligated sya now with that wuestion maam ni I can say that it must be work with hand and hand with both division and the school because mayroon din silang fault at fault dyan in a sense na matagal sya ma release ang kwarta that is why once mag mask na ng liquidation deffinetly at the end pa pud sya maliquidate sa isa ka school head, now in abase of our experienced maam nahatag ang kwarta is December so how could we able to buy things pa within month kung one month lang nan aa pay mga sugan a iliquidate so I think because of this maam no ma address din sya also sa dapat pud I address especially to the higher up actually we open that one already and one thing for sure kay diba kay legal basis kasi ang pag babase dyan when we talk about 9184 meron nakalagay doon talaga nap ag ma receive mo na ang money 15 days dapat mo talaga ma liquidate sya or one month that's why mo adhere man ta ana so lisod pud sya as kabahin sa school head kay we don't any choice explain our side kay kung muingon me ug ana na dugay sya nahatg ang kwarta mu sanga sanga sya dugay man pud mo nag ask ug request na dugay request kay tungod na murag ana sya maam jul. but again and again how to solve of that one maam no I think as a school head we need to plan tanan mga needed requirements especially sap ag request kasi meron syang mga step by step when you have the RCA or shall I say the request of cash advance. Number 1 is you will start it with asking for the request that is request from the teachers or even sa imong office that must be followed by pag naay request na you will have o to consolidate na to canvass after na canvass Ninyo is you will have the resolution kung kinsa ang nanalo and kung kinsa tung nanalo that's the time you will have the PO the purchase order and that purchase order is very much important maam jul it is because it is an agreement of the store and the school, now kung mo baba or mutaas man ang presyo kung unsa ang napermahan Ninyo mao jud na in the event na wa silay mahatag pwede nimo sila kasohan if you will read that one PO what's the purpose of having PO so meaning ana that is a document that would proved kung pila inyoha unsay mga nasabutan Ninyo given the period of time after the PO that's the time you will pay but you cannot pay without the received money from the division office if you are an non ayo or non-implementing unit so that would be a kuan jul no lisod jud sya karon even karon di jud sya ma sulbad sulbad up to this base we haven't receive yet our RSA for the first quarter what time is it what month it is last month of the quarter so it would be very difficult for us so thank you and good afternoon.

- JOANA MAE ROJAS

I agree with sir Jeson no kay tama wala pa ang amoang RCA niabot so kanang amoang cluster head mag sige na ingon na pag naa na ang budget pag dali ta jo mag abtik ta jo Hala oi pwede maluya nya karon gihatag nya pagkahuman next week dapat mag liquidate na daw ko hala kakapoy kahangak ba ana gud. Pero tama pud jud to si sir jeson na unta ang division mapapaspas pud nila para kami pud na naa diri sa school dili pud me mag lisod so mao to sya.

- **JESON**

  Jul taysa jul I think it will not be avoided ay ma avoid sya but I think 1% sya ha for me the propability of ma avoid sya is just 1% though maingon ta nganong mabuhat sa uban because sa atoang school we are are all 484 eh for example ha 500 pala tayo na school dito so in terms of pag manage palang daan sa pagsulod sa kwarta sa pag check sa report madugay dugay jud sya until such time na maabtan jud ka ug number of days nga an9g im9uha daw kay sayo ka nga nag pasa wala pa sya na check isa lang ka mali I agree with maam lisari kuan ganina statement nga kung even erasure sya bawal sya ipatawag pa jud sya so samot syag madugay jul especially karon pud ha because you base it 2021 no the covid 19 has also kuan no kaning affect us on terms of liquidation kay ang signaturies wala ang mag check ana sya jul. but al least one thing I would like to emphasize on how to avoid this one is kuan lang siguro jud sayohon nalang ang tanan both ends the division at the same time the school head right at role iya jud syang buhaton.

  I think maam jul voice out na sya since then pa nahitabo na sya however in terms of kuan as a new kuan wala kaau ko ka feel ug kanang kumbaga technical assistance regarding with that if unsaon jud sya namo dili ko ka kuan ha pero so far ha sa akong experience wala man japun again and again repitedly kuan sya done.

- **LISARIE BARGAYO**

  Dili ko ka relate maam kay karon lang man gud kadungog aning mga unobligated amount. Unya wa pud koy MOOE pud so murag dili lang sa ko muistorya kung unsa pa gyud ana kay wala kay wala pa koi statement.

- **MARLON PAUL**

  Daghan kog obligations wala koy unobligated.

- **JESON**

  Wala silay unobligated jul because they don't have yet the MOOE sir marlon the unobligated term is used to those who received RCA for the last quarter na wala pa nimo na kuan. That's why na mention to sa atoang school kato gung gi giingon ni sir Jan if ive mention name but I will not mention the school katong wala pa na liquidate and you cannot accept another RCA once you are not yet done with your previous requested budget.

c. Being a novice school head, how do you find the guidelines and system that were being implemented by the central office and division office with regards to MOOE? **44:28**

- **JESON**

  Okay regarding with that system no we cannot question that one because its already in the implementing rules and regulations and we can research that one to republic act 9184 that it talks abput the MOOE so that we cannot kuan talaga question in terms of the system but if we have time to change it or if we can suggest to change it definitely daghan kaau maka-ingon na usabon unta sya pero into systems jud sya I cannot understand the point into systems, so the written po ba yung anong flow or katong modification nga unsay pamaagi sa division. Can I ask again sa researcher kung unsay gina mean nimo maam jul?

Ah okay so it means that nakalagay talag sya sa implementing rules and regulation na kasi dyan jul you cannot question that one pag nakalagay sya sa republic act atchaka sa process ng system . if we have kasi I love your topic no. if we have time to read 9184 I believed that you've included that one in your RRL kindly include that one the 9184 naa dadto sya naka state no in terms of system how to do MOOE but if dito lang sa atin no for example the number of days kung dapay dalion nila ana lang sya pero we cannot question kasi about the person kung ikuan nato sya into CI like iinvestigate nato . who are at fault with that no ngano madugay sya but as to system jul dili kaau sya ing.ana ka direct ma change kay tungod naan na sya.

Ah of course improve is kuan man gyud sya no dynamic man gyud ang improve that means naa gyud na sya ang improvement I mean. But okay sya ang system ha okay man sya ang system walay kuan kay correctness man kay we are dealing with money financial ang pinaguusapan maganda man ang system okay sya ganito ang proceso kasi pero madugay lang ka tungod lang sa . di man gud ta pwede manisi ug tao no na involved na dugay sya mo approve kana man gud ang concern dira ang approval man gud na kung dali lang to sya na tatakan unta na release na unta ang kwarta wala man problema ang system okay man ma follow man namo nga mao ni unahon pero dili pud pwede sisihon man gud si tao ngano ana so ana lang siguro sya maam jul.

- **LISARIE**

Naa man gud toy sir jeson basin maka explain sya ba kay wala man gud kaau na though naminaw ko pero dili kaau nako sya ma relate kay tungod wala man gud me MOOE kato ganing last nato webinar gani sir jeson I guess atong murag is ato sa mga system na gusto nilang I implement para kunuhay madali ang kuan I do not know kung pa gyuy ma. Unsa gyuy maau adto kuan sir sa system nato karon sa liquidation kay wa kaau ko naka seryoso ad2.

JESON

Oo okay to sya nga system maam Lisarie katong iencode nalang ana nalang sya pero kung. I ask kasi maam Julie the researcher kung unsa iyang pasabot na system. Pero kato sya na systema okay nato sya naga improve man gyud sya no nga instead of ascending then naa nay iagi nlang through sending ana gud no na mo check nalang me even pag ad2 sa landbank dili naman me muad2 sa landbank to ask pila among kwarta nalang nabilin sa kuan diba maam joan? dili nata muad2 sa landbank kay naa natoy mga ilandbank na ito nalang I kuan mo download nalang sa atoag kuan papers ing.ana sya. So okay pud sya malipay me ana jul kung mapadayun lami na si sir marlon ang muperma sa approval.

Sa region sya

LISARIE

Para mapadali ang mga transaction mao na ilang pinakabag.o na system karon gina ano.

d. What are the factors that you need to consider in handling school finances? **49:48**

- **JOANA**

  Ang mga factors need nimo I consider syempre dapat kadtong mga SIP nimo imohang APP, PPMP dapat naka align na sya pareha namo karon ang amoang problema naa me gusto na ipabuhat however pag check diay namo sa APP pag pa canvass nako nya pag wala sya so isa jud diay to sa factor na dapat namo I work out then karon nag ingon na dili sa daw pwede ang repair so mga sunod pa na quarter and then mag re align me sunod quarter pa pud so mao to sya ang kailangan jud nimo I consider na dapat naka align ang imohang katong mga SIP APP para ma

  you: so youre saying maam na it should be planned well para align.

  yes kana mao jud sya dapat.

- **LISARIE**

  Kato maam planning gyud kung unsa ang imohang gi plano stick to it though naa kay mga modification na himoon pero atleast mainly nan aa naka naka han.ay na nimo for a year. Ikaduha gyud na pinakaimportante icondsider is ang time kana bang pag set nimo pag plas-tar nimo sa time kanus.a. kasi ang time man gud iimpose nimo sa imong kaugalingon as a school head. Dili nimo sya iimpose lang didto sa imohang mga teachers kay magkinaunsa magkinaunsa ma late ang imohang kaning about aning imohang liquidation sa imo man gud gihapon padulong so ang akong pasabot is kanang ang time timeline ang pag kuan nimo is importante gyud kau say kay sayo lanh man gyud tong himoon tung uban didto lang man gyud mamoblema sa kanang ma late ka ana gud dili nimo sya ma comply sa time na gihatag nila didto magka problema gyud.

- **MARLON**

  Kuan lang man wala man kaau koy school finances gud I just have to kuan lang be transpar-ent on what coming in na mga sponsor mga money ako lang isulti sa mga teachers na ing. ana kay kuan lang man ang importante karon kay makahatag lang me modules and SLM sa mga bata mao lang mana sya and then kung nay bisita naa me pakaon. Nevertheless actually kana gung school finances magamit mo kasi yan sa ano brigada and ASP kasi we need to kuan man gud upload In the DPDS so magamit gihapon tung mga kwarta na mga ginapanghatag sa amoa. Even ukay ukay ako na syang I considered as sponsor so naa gi-hapon syay corresponding na amount para ma upload nila sa DPDS kay one of the criteria nga murag dako ang imohang kana ganing outside gani na mga money na nisulod sa imong skwelahan.

- **JESON**

  I would like to add on with the considerations no in the factors to consider in handling school finances so it was mentioned by maam Joana the planning the second one it was mentioned ni maam Lisarie as well the third one is sir Marlon about the transparency I agree with that because that's why we are required to have a transparency board . I would like to add with the word accountability and it would also address to the answer of maam lisarie earlier about unsa pa ang mali imo syang accountable ka tanan that's why dili jud dapat mag uban si supply ug si MOOE incharge kay pwede niya I kuan because kung unsay ni perma dira whatever money you've received accountable ka ana that's why we have this fidelity bond mao na sya ang purpose sa fidelity bond para ma determe kinsa ang accountable officer kung unsa man ang mahitabo sya jud ang signatory ana then it really need also to think about accountability maam Julie.

e. when it becomes to school needs, differentiate your level of concerns now that you are the school head compared when you were once a teacher?

- **JESON**

  When it becomes to school heads no if you will have the scale with 1-10 I believe that the level of the differentiation of being a teacher and a school head I guess I could give 10 kay layo gyud kaau sya because in terms of sa KRA the key results area our focus of being a teacher is just to each if we will just want to think about the basic just to teach just to give information but as to school head noe your KRA is not just merely to teach kasi part nya ang teaching no the learning and teaching process but you have a different domains na to consider namely: leading strategically managing operations and resources focusing in teaching and learning that why we have observation number 4 is developing self we need to attend program but we need also to develop others that is why developing self and others and of course yung ginagawa ni sir markon at ni maam lisarie having topping stakeholders that is building connections so that's why I can give from 1-10 jul. no in terms of differentiation again I will give 10.

- **JOANA**

  Layo pud jud kaau sya no kay tama to sya si sir Jason na if teacher lang ka ang mga needs sa classroom sa imong mga students mga output ang mga lesson na imong dapat I prepair ang mga subject coordinators nimo but when you become a school head mas dako ang imuhang respondibility and ikaw jud ang pinaka accountable nga tao dinha sa school and it's a very big responsibility like for example nay mali imohang teacher dili man gyud deritso ang teacher ang pangutan.on ikaw man gyud mismo so mao gyud na ang permente gina ingon nila if kanang naam oy mga gusto kanang naam oy mga projects or mga dapat buhaton please iinform gyud ko Ninyo kay at the end of the say I will be the one accountable so mag differ gyud sya sa accountability so mag bug.at gyud ang sa school head kay sa school head dala pa nimo ang mga stakeholders ang pa mower sa skwelahan ang kuryente sa skwelahan so imuha gyud na tanan plus lahi lahi pa gyud ang demand sa teachers and you canot please every teacher na naa ka mao to sya jul.

- **MARLON**

Okay sa as for me no about the level of concerns theirs huge different between the teachers and the school head of course the level of concerns same with Sir Jeson kumbaga 101 ang intensity ana sa kana ganing difference it is because as a school head you need to maintain a role as a role model of the community you will be accountable of everything your school is your shield your pedestal kay you have to maintain a good image a harmonious relationship with the community because if someone of the group in the community will not trust you of course It will have a domino effect. And kasi pag teacher ka you don't have any concern you're the four walls of your classroom your students and even you don't have the hell I care I will post this I will comment something against the government I don't care im just a teacher im not a school head. But then when you are already a school head you areaccountable you are have the responsibility everything goes with your image but if kana ganing naay mga lapses or short coming no you can overcome it but once na you commit mistakes It will be forever be kuan gani kanang remembered mga goodness nimo pahapyaw nalang na pero once na you commit mistakes as a school head it will be forever be remembered that is why you have to be careful you don't have to be careless you have to be careful all the time you maintain your image kung ang image ko kasi ako kasi ako I'm a social blonder or kasi as a school head I have to be im not against about changing your image ha teacher palang ako sa sped ganito na talaga itsura ko I wear jewelries and then brown na akong hair kasi it's a traditionally I have to maintain and proper short hair cut hair not comparing to sur jeson ha kay ing.anajud na iyang personal very formal gyud na sya pero ako man gud kay kana ganing if you know how to carry yourself ana lang sya panindigan ra nimo so as to you are also accountable to your image as long as you will be trusted ang imong itsura kanang dili ka kuan dili ka mangingilad sometimes man gud ko kanang kabalo ko mo encourage people dili sa pagpangilad na but to encourage people to help you dili pud na sya atik atik you need to be honest all the time mao na sya na its part of our aura mao na sya nag accountability responsibility and transparency as a leader of the school no mao na tung giingon ni sir jeson no yung katong 5 domains ba to it is strategically, managing school operation para ma memorize nako ba developing others focusing teaching and learning and building connection with which is I am very much kana ganing forte ko kasi kana ganing ako man gud panlaban gud. when I was in sped bangkal ako pud ang grabe ug connections kay ang akoang panlaban kay ang special children kay ako man gud ang kana gung head sa IDD intellectual disability department and I know how to encourage people to help the special children ing.ana dili sad na pagpangilad pero in find to help the special education na needs children na kailangan nila ug kanang mga assessment na naa man gud childen na wala na assist so assist ug tarong dili sila diagnosed properly so kailangan nila sponsor to pay the development sa pediatrician so nagka hinay hinay na mga linkages gidala pud nako didto sa akoang bukid sa IP community so akong pung panglaban sa akaong pag encourage sa people to help us is the IP community. Ako man gud is a marketing graduate former lang ko sa education so medyo kabalo mo ing.ana.

- **LISARIE**

Ako didto kato kay sir na kung iyahang I record scale ng 1-10 ang difference is 10 gyud kana bitawng as a school head man gud kana bang mangita kag problema kay sulbaron nimo ang problema kana gud unya katong kauban nimo na nangitag problema sila pud diay tuy usahay naay problema murag ing.ana ba its not just kaning pag teacher man gud ka ang imohang man gud is magtudlo ka sa mga bata something ingon ana lang ba pero pag once naa na ang school head naka dili lang bata ang imohang concern though ang end nimo is ang bata but makita nimo as a school head na usahay maam dili gyud nimo makita gyud ang problema the way si school head mutan.aw sa isa ka though pareho mo ug skwelahan everyday ga kuyog mo pero lahi ang pantlantaw ni teacher sa iyahang skwelahan ug lahi pud ang perspective ni school head pag mag tan.aw sya sa iyahang skwelahan because again kana bang dili ang end nimo is bata pero tanwon diay nimo nga nganong ingon ani man ang bata ay kay si teacher naa pud diay syay problema murag ana ba and you have to address also that as a school head dili mana nimo sya pasagdahan diba? Tas ay naay problema si bata ay ang iyaha diayng ginikanan kay ang family niya ang naay problema so mangita na pud ka pamaagi so diha ana gani maammangita na pud ka pamaagi kung un-saon na pud nimo tung family usahay ti the extent nga usahay si community pag gyud diay ang naay problema which is dako na gyud sya kaau. Kanang siguro sakto. Ako sa una man gud katong teacher pa gyud ko kanang daghan kog dili masabtan sa way sa mga school head before that it why kanang kasagaran sa akong mga school head masuklan gyud na nako murag ana ba kanang malditahan ana gud though I know gyud na dili jud good ang ilahang perception sa akoa because to me ako sa akong end wala ko kasabot pasabta ko murag something ingon ana ba because as a teacher limitado lang gyud ang imong panlan-taw pag naa ka sa school so mao na sya kay limitado man imong pagsabot sa school kay gamay lang man ang imuhang gina lantaw na tao mao nan ga gamay lang pud ang imohang mubo lang pud ang imohang level of concern pero pagka school head naka magkataas ang imuhang magkadako magkalapad ang imohang panlantaw ang imuhang perspective ug ang katong mabati gyud nimo nga unsa gyud diay nang direction no organizational direction and goal dira nimo makita ang kadaghan sa problema and mas mutaas ang imuhang level of concern. So layo ra jud sya kaau maam

Yes. Kanag outright na reaction. Muingon gyud ko na ay nganong kuan mani oi murag ing. ana ba pero sa akoa man gud na sitwasyon I really never I did not apply for the position ac-tually nag uli na gyud ko sa akoang mother school I already gave up the school kaning Nor-berto national high school kumbaga gibiyaan na nako na sila so ibig sabihin the thought of kaning mahimo kung school head ako na na syang gi let go at that time pero after 6 months murag ana ba gi kanang naay order naay task na gipahimo nako for that school gihimo nako sya nga wala ko nibalik sa skwelahan nagpabilin ko sa akoang mother school pero akoa to syang gi trabaho hangtod niabot ang time na kinahanglan na gud ko mubalik because I have I was desiccated as the teacher in charge as the school head so mao ng naana ko para sa akoa is para bang is this di kaning path na para sa ako for ing.aan na pud ang akong hunahuna na dili na gyud sya kaau kanang bang mura bag kanang ako syang gi desire but something na akong gi realize na it's a call for me so siguro sa akoa I do not know within the people na naa sa akoang palibot kung naa pa guy trust naa pa guy silay Nakita sa akoa kay para sa akaoang kaugalingon wala lang kabalo lang gyud ko nga kanang supakira ko mao ra gyud nang akong nabal.an but ana ra gyud say maam mao nan ga karon nga pag naa koi problem mao na sya nga hearing from my colleague pud sa cluster six na mag TMPM muingon ra gyud silage tagam merisi nganong ni enter nga ana ba nihilak ka pero mukatawa ra pud ka magkadugay bitaw nga wa bitaw nag sugo pwede ra gyud inatawn.

2. How do they cope with the challenges or obstacles as fiscal managers? **1:08:48**

a. who are the people that has been helping you function well as fiscal manager? What kind of help they have already extended to you in this matter?

- **JESON**

  Okay in terms of the first question no who are the people since the department of education in terms of style of leadership we are bureaucracy meaning bureaucratic that means there are people talaga higher than us na maau atong adtuan in terms of asking help so if we will go back to kuan jul no na system jud sa department of education if you are a school head definitely you must be assisted with the technical with the PSDS in terms of the technical assisteance or maybe from the division office to our education program supervisor or even in the regional office ana lang sya maam jul no so mao lang na sya akoang I kuan I will not mention others nalang kay because that is to kuan na no ofcourse naa man gyud ang tao all around us but as to system of the department of education definitely the PSDS the the division office and the region office

- **JOANA**

  I agree with sir Jeson no of course our PSDS but and also my cluster MOOE cluster supervisor also sa mga people daghan jud kaau ug mga tao nga naka help sa akoa no and one of them also is my former school head sya pud ang isa sa nag recommend sa akoa na maging teacher in charge si Maam doren aglizamendez and kanang mga principals pud na mas season, season principals and even us kami na mga peers no kami diri sa cluster six mag tinabangay me so mao na sya ang mga tao na nakapa help sa amoa na to really manage our school kung unsay mga problema kami ra puy mag sinumbungay ug kami ra puy mag tinabangay.

- **LISARIE**

  Okay pagkakaron ang Nakita nako na mag help sa akoa isa kaning ADAS kay sila man ang nakabalo sa kanang mga templates tanan tanan mga gamiton ang of course ang property custodians so far sa akong estado karon maam mao pa na sila aside from sir jeson nga permenente jud na sila naa dira and maam joana and sir marlon sangpiton lang jud na biski pa alas onsi sa gabie tubag jud na sya dayon.

- **MARLON**

Ako pud in terms of fiscal nga fiscal nga about money me myself and I wala man gud kay. Acyually man gud ko naga. Im not lifting my own chair ha basta ako man gud kung kaya ko kayanin ko nalang kaysa pag ma because kana ganing rejection is a very kanang very sad to accept no its not an easy thing to accept kanang rejection because I was being rejected by many times kana ganing magpa help ka so wala puy gina rely na lain na tao kundi akoang sarili in terms of fiscal ha were talking about fiscal in other matters I can rely to people trusted people like PSDS especially maam alma kay belong man ko before sa elementary karon nabuyan naman gud ko nag hinay hinay lang gyud nako syag condition sa iyang self nan aa gyud ko sa cluster 6 kay ang aoa man gud I have to protect my teachers kay elementary man gyud sila so dili ko kapangayo ug items sa elementary kung dili ko magkuan pud did-to sa PSDS elementary so nakakuha naman ko isa ka teacher sa kinder so okay nako sa highschool na pud ko na magayo ug high school teacher kay wala man ko teacher so ang ako pang isa ka pang isa ka teacher nag hatag sa among school kaming duha so in terms of fiscal kami lang mga teachers ako kanang kuan man gud kat dili ko gusto ug storya storya man gud about money gani kanang basi kanang sige kog paamot dige kog paamot mga ana gud dili ko ganahan ana makadungog so rather kuan kanang do it myself alone so kanang kumbaga kaya pa nako pwede ako kanang I kuan pero ug dili gyud kaya I need the support of the teachers so I am just telling them na okay lang ba na mag kuan ta naa baya tay mga ana naa tay mga situation na kailangan so hopefully dira na nako mahibalan no na as fiscal managers if the time comes the time for me is that they will be given a MOOE so diha na nako mahibal.an na how will I function well as fiscal manager

b. What are the learning programs that really equip you in handling school reasurces?

- **JOAN**

Unsa sya na learning programs jul?

You: any learning programs you've attended to like webinars naa bas regions

Ah oo syempre o naa jud na sya katong latest namo na webinar katong about sa new handling sa MOOE kato sya jul. pero mostly man gud hands on man jud sa hands on dinha jud ka maka learn . kay usahay dili kaau ko kasabot sa webinar pero pag abot na sa ano sa pagsulbad sa problema kay anaon diay na sya naa diay pina anaon ra diay to. Kay taas kaau sila iexplain so mas makalearn ko sa hands on siguro ana pud ko na learner

- **LISARIE**

Learning program gawas sa mga leadership siguro no mga webinars na training kaning about sa kaning curriculum and instruction and of course kanang kana bitawng mga program ah ambot lang maam ha kay galibog man gud ko anang Deped maam oi malibog man ko aning ilahang. Mao ning program pagabot did2 sa ubos ay timesa timesa asa mani dapit I bangga atong gi trabaho diri something ingon ana ba. Siguro ako lang ang wla kasabot nga ing.anaon lang diay na siya pero as of karon murag what are the learning programs that they could be handling school resources training mga training sa SIP mga ingon ana kay dira man gud ang pag handle man gud sa resources depende sa imong plano and ang tanan man gud na resources naka kuan sya naka achor sya sa imong SIP which is actually SIP is kaning unsay tawag ana kanang imohang plan imohang vision man pud gud sya. Murag ana ba wala kaau ka nag hisgot did2 ug kanang sa SIP wala kaau ka nag hisgot ug kwarta did2 pero pag imo syang I breakdown ang ending niya kay kwarta murag ana ba resources ang kinahanglan para ma achieve nimo tung imohang plan did2 imohang improvement plan ana.

YOU: so far maam with the training that you have mention maam you have attended before, where those trainings enough po or kulang pa gyud?

Trainings are good trainings are kaning very relevant ang kulang lang sa ako sa ako lang ha maam ha kulang lang ang kaning time and monitoring na gihatag sa ibabaw para namo ma practice ba para makita namo asa ang amoang kakayahan asa ang dili namo kaya with regards to kanang ilahang training na ilahang gihatag kanang tungod bas a kapaspas siguro maam daghan kaau sila gi download na mga training or unsa pa na dinha unya na mahulog na mamubo na gud kaau ang ang time namo para among ma simulate no or among ma practice to and para sa akoa pareho kay maam joana na mas Makaton mas mag stay man gud ang learning style nako maam ba kanang mas makasabot ko kung gina lihok nako ang murag ana maam ba so ing.ana ang akong concern kulang lang ta I do not know pud sa uban kung unsa pud ang ilahang kuan.

- **JESON**

Same thing with them jul, I've attended latest seminar regarding a with resources but for me kung enough ba sya or dili sya enough. Dili sya enough pa since naa pa me sa 3 years and below pa me halos tanan sa amoang kuan jud sa amoang experience so hopefully looking forward for more seminars regarding with regading on how to handle resources thank you.

- **MARLON**

Yeah actually even katong teacher pa yata ko na nag kuan nako mga learning programs na leadership trainings, how to handle school, how to handle finances in school. Ive been attending that because I cannot they will not permit me to take the exam if you dont have a leadership seminar its part of the requirement kasi so you need to know the basics let's start the basic. So as mentioned no SIP is the road map for 3 years sa school 2-3 years or 3-4 years ana sya so SIP would be yours stating board as to looking for if you want to be equip in school resources kasi you need to have funds no kanang school improvement plan so as to kuan pud and then actually all the school heads were kanang were given a chance to have a training yung mga new mga untrained school heads for k-12 program so part of it im sure that there will be topic on school resources how to handle school finances so were looking forward actually nag butang na me akoa si sir jeson si maam lisarie did2 sa link nato. So kana naa me mga trainings soon sa mga untrained mga novice mga new fight na mga school head.

Part of it man gud na kana ganing medyo akoa kanang ganing tung unsa kay hala oi dili ko gusto mag kanang cluster kay puro sila high school now ive kanang experienced yesterday sa amoang mura syag team building kay nag kinataw.anay me murag ganahan na oud kanang hala oi lami man diay sila kaubanon so ikaw pud na murag madasig pud ka bam o encourage. Pero kana ganing I can blend with any people man gud I can blend with any walks of life ana man gud wala man gud koy kuan ako lang kay kanang medyo ano lang ko usahay kanang akong personality kay aryat aryat man gud ko so oi basin dili ko mag blend in sa ilaha na group pero ive discovered no sa ilaha pud kay kana man gud kay its one way of kana ganing exchanges exchanging of ideas man gud sa mga school heads labi na tung mga season principal mga PHD na mga principal daghan silag mga natun.an pa sa ilang kinabuhi unsa being a school head kana man gud in that way in that kind of event man gud daghan kag matun.an sa ilaha so ikaw pud ma dasig gyud ka no ma enhance ang imong pagka school head though ako mura gyud kog britisian na school head kay kana lagi kong ako mura ug gikan kog manicure nag manicure ko sa kuan ana ko ka flamboyant. So ing.ana ko day ang akong personality so ana pud no so enjoy enjoy sya just enjoy yourself kaning equip with many skills no upskilling kumbaga so upskilling reskilling dili pud mag downskilling no mao nana ang hawa resign na lang resign nalang sa serbisyo kung wan aka ganahi.

c. As to what extent where you able to explore in addressing school concerns?

- **LISARIE**

As to what extent where you able to explaore in addressing school concerns kuan pa sya kanang dili pa gyud kaau nako kanang nahimo ang tanan or or pasabot wala pa gyud nako na explore ang tanan Nakong pwedi himoon to address school concern as of karon maam kay gamay pa man ang amoang problem kana bang ang pag address nako sa mga concerns nako sa school is kanang tung kutob sa akong nahimo palang wala pa ko nag go beyond sa uncomfortable zone kumbaga naa pako sa akong comfort zone in addressing school concerns siguro tungod siguro kay bag.o pa maam murag ana ba gamay pa kong makit.an na problema naa koi mga nakit.an na mga siguro gamay ang problema pero nakit.an na nako na in the long run dapat masulbad n ani na problema kung ingon ani dapat akong buhaton murag ingon ana pa maam ba so wala pa kaau ko ninggawas sa akoang comfort zone to kuan to explore na ,ga butang na mutubag sa kuan sa pagkakaron maam wala pa kaau.

- **JOAN**

Makarelate jud ko sa pinaka latest kay 2 months naman gud ang amoang electricity unya naguol ko ba kay naa me experienced ana before nga naputlan gyud ang eskwelahan dili ako ang school head si tung previous nako na school head na putlan gyuf me nya kanang naa man diay na reconnection pay no pagkahuman murah nigasto yata me ato na time ug naa sa mag 10000 ug Nakita gyud nako akoang school head ato ba na problemado kaau sya unya ako nalang puy nag initiate atong nga kanang mag amot amot nalang teachers kung pila atong maamot ako pa juy nagpatawag sa mga ano mga parents that's time na mag help ba na kanang murag 35 pesos lang gud na amot ana gud sya para lang gyud maka help ko sa akoang school head at that time so everytime na muaabot na gyud ug 2 months ang amoang electricity murag ma panic ko ma pressure ko ba kay dili nako gyud gusto ma-hitabo sa akoang time na maputlan ang skwelahan ug kuryente so since wala pa man ang amoang request ay wala pa man ang amaoang budget niabot so tapal sa jud ana lang gyud so hopefully ingon man sila sir arvie na ma reimburse lang man sya so ana gyud ang atoang accountability no kanang unta kwarta jud unta dapat ang school head kay para dali ra kaau ikatapal ba ana pero sige lang kay God will provide lang man gihapon and also kanang re-solving conflict kana gyud ang akong isa sa mg ana learn as a school head kay naa gyuy time na kanang imohang teacher dili ganahan sa imoha masking para sa imo wala gud kay gihimo na dautan pero para sa iya murag naa gyud syay maingon na something is wrong with you so dili ko ganahan gyud ug conflict actually pero pag school head diay ka wala kay choice you need to resolve some conflict so isa sa akoang extent na gibuhat kay kalevel lang gud me sa years ba na nag ano me na nag start dinha so syempre ang seniority namo both no muag ang familiarity naa so I really need to confront her unsa gyud imong problema ana gani as murag nidle ko as a friend and as also a school head so ing ana kailangan jud nako sya I resolve ang conflict face to face dili sya pwede na gi istoryahan lang nako ah gi storya nako sa lain sya gyud akong dapat storyahon ana gani and also the same sa mga stakeholders kay naa gyud mga stakeholders pud na dili ganahan sa imoha abi nako pag school head ka ganahan tanan ang tao sa imo dili diay so you also need to address ba nga sila gyud mismo ang imong storyahon kay kablo naka sa mga barangay storya did2 ana. So mao to sya jul mao to akong mga extent sa akong and kanan pung mag hauling kung walay mo haul sa module e ikaw pag haul ana gud grabe jud mura rag dili mura rag sayon so grabe murag imong panuhot tanan ma feel gyud nimo oh tanang aspects so kato lang jul

- **JESON**

Asme answer with them ko jul pero kato gud maam jo katong regarding sa imong concerns kapag maputlan pwede ra gud ra mo mag letter sa kuan ana maam jo sa Davao light mag letter lang mo kay base sa rollings kay dili man makaputol kay public pag government con-nection sya so all you gonna do is to informing them.pero mao lang lagi sya ulaw lang sya pero sige lang I email. May pag mag letter nalang mo jo kay para dili mo maputlan ana ra man sya.

LISARIE

Sir jeson mag letter ka sa DLPC nga public institution mo?

- **JESON**

 Dili nga madugay ka bayad. Understood man daan nga public institution kay mo reflect baya ang name sa school diba? Nakabuhat ko ka isa kay katong dugay gyud pero okay ra man nabaik lang man gihapon wa man naputlan.

d. there are times that the requested monthly/quarterly MOOE are delayed and you have a so many needs in that specific time. How were you able to compose yourself and remain optimistic in this kind of situation?

- **JESON**

We don't have any choice man to look beautiful in the eyes of many man gyud no lain pud kaau jul no na you are the head you are the best a visual aid for the teachers and the community yet kuan kaau ka tan.awon haggard. Mao lang jul as If lang na nothing happens mao lang jud sya ang imong buhaton no pero behind that happiness, behind that success or behind that mile there are a lot of kuan no pinagdaanan nimo nga challenges ive experience na nakaaway gyud nako akong accountant. Ang giingon sa akoa kay among all the school na iyang na meet ako daw nag pinakapamati and I don't care kay mali man pud gud to iyahang point kasi dili man gud sya pwede gud jul na I change rag kalit ang imohang request it is because lahi ang na release na kwarta ako jud ang mo adjust so murag ing.ana gud sya pero wala tay mabuhat kundi go work lang gihapon kay naa man sa system no bread and butter man nato sya unless kong business man ko dugay nako nihawa but we still love I chose to still love my work and the department of education that's why okay ra jul ana lang ang life ana ra gud oi thank you.

YOU: so the key there sir is your love for the school.

Oo mao na ang imohang theme na buhaton sa imong research mao na ang imong thematic analysis.

YOU: love and ano pud setting the right mindset.

- **JOANA**

Especially katong nag start ang pandemic daghan kaau mga kulang no kulang bondpaper kailangan ni so ofcourse you need to tap mag binaga jud kag nawng para lang gyud naay bondpaper ang skwelahan so I tap nimo ang imong mga kaila mga friend stakeholders ana jud as a leader you need to be quick thinker man pud gud tas kanang dpaat maka decide ka pero dapat paspas ka mag9 decide pero at the same time wise pud imong decisions so kailangan nimo sya e balance no and how do I remain optimistic in this kind of situation?kanang ano lang gyud kanang salig lang ko mao gyud na akoang sig lang ko na masulbad lang gyud tanang problem ana sagubangon sa skwelahan 9kay if I keep on worrying wala man gihapon ma help akong pag worries so I pray nlang nako na I help ko sa ginoo. Ay isa siay na sa akong gina pray perme ug pinaka importante gyus na prayer para sa akoa is hatagn jdu ug wisdom kay ang knowledge man gud sometimes dili gyud nato masaligan no pero if its wisdom form the Lord especially if kanang mga lisod na mga problema na mura mag tama pero dili mani tama murag ana gud so you need to really pray for wisdom and to trust na everything will be okay all is well.

- **LISARIE**

Wala gyud kay choice as a school head diba no basta leader gyud ka mam wala gyud na na kuan kanang unsay tawag ani naa pa ba kay wa gyud kay choice sa in the middle sa negative kanang negative na situation kung ang tanang negatibo ikaw nalnag gyud magpabiling optimistic sa tinood lang dili gyud ka pwede magpadala ma negative but in the middle of kaning positive na kanang sitwaasyon kanang good ang tanan you should be the one to the first one to think about what would be the negative aning ka positive ani na sitwasyon ikaw ang pinakaunan mag huna huna nga there might me something wrong ana gihapon mura syag maam ba kanang sa military maam ba sa tactical operation ba kanang kung hilom kaau ayaw jud pag huna huna ug okay na diba pag hilom gani kaau pag good kaau ang dagan mag hunahuna na gyud ka kung hangtod as ani kutob ang kahilom ang positive sa sitwasyon and what eoukd be the kaning what would be the kaning cause ng pinakaunang chaos ani something ingon ana because you have really to plan kay pag abot ana na kanang naa jud diay syay negative na consequence ikaw naka plan ahead naka unsa ang positive na himoon nimo so at the time na negative na ang tanan ikaw nalang ang nagpabiling positive because you already have have seen imomg na ng Nakita na kanang pagiging visionary so ang skill maam sa isa ka school head is kuan kanang skill gyud sya na kabalo ka mutan. aw sa positive diha sa negative na sitwasyon siba maam oh kanang tanan na gyud na negative pero na kitan pa gyup na ops blessing in these guys is true and this is it ana jud sya tinood gyud na sya maam and as a school head dapat naa gyud ka ana imo gyung nang gunitan sa imohang heart.

e. what are your best pratices as to overcoming the obstacles of being the school fund manager?

- **JOANA**

  One best practices namo is to really collaborate no especially sa amoang cluster ad at the same time blessed pud ko na naa koi isa ka teacher na kabalo na pud sya na mas hawd pud sya sa akoa sa paghimog request makahelp sya sa akoa sa liquidation kay before murag gina akoa ra man gud nako tanan ana gud so bug.at man diay pag akoon nimo tanan so you delegate dili pud I delegate tanan but you are partnering ba maam jo unsa ni atoang kailangan buhaton unsa diay imong plano maam? naa lagi lagi mangutana sa akoa ana so happy ra pud ko na na a partnering and collaboration gyud with your teacher and your cluster.

- **LISARIE**

  Kuan akoa plan ahead. Kay aron dili ka sigeg laban miski wala ka kalaban because at that time na laban kang wala kay kalaban actually ang imong kalaban dira isa ang time nimo wala na jud kay wala na kay time so plan ahead para ma organized pa nimo ang mga butang na kung naa man galling dili mahitabo as plan gamay nalang gyud sya kaaung changes imong himoon dili ka madugay so ing.ana lang sya

- **JESON**

  Same thing with them delegation coordination and plan and monitoring and evaluation so ako nalang gi kuan jul gi isa isa thank you.

3. what are the insights that can be drawn from this study? **1:38:32**

a. as school head, how do you establish your authority as fiscal manager?

- **JOANA**

How do I establish my authority ano jud sya you need to walang personalan lang ingana gud walang personalan kasi shes just my friend for the longest time pud I consider her as my friend and katong pagabot na na naging school head nako lahi maam lahi na akoang concerns ana gud so I need kailangan jud ko na as a leader man gud dili pasabot na ako ang pinakataas ug position dinha meaning ana ikaw gyud dapat masunod so you need also to go down to the level dapat ikaw ang pinaka broad sa tanang teachers sa tanang tao diri ikaw ang pinaka broad ug mind and ako lang gyud ginaano is basta wala koi gi basta akong motive and akoang intention are for the benefit for the school students and community then I could esetablish my authority so as long as wala koi ginaapakan nga tao and naga sunod lang pud ko sa mga deped orders.

- **LISARIE**

Ako kuan siguro pinakauna dapat as kaning fiscal manager kanang ikaw ang mag initiate no ug kanang pagpaabot sa imohang kaning subordinates or miskin sa community ana bang kanang accountability and transparency ba dili ka maghulat nga naa pay mag complain sa imuha nga bago nimo na ipagawas ang mga dapat nimong ipagawas so mangita sila ug dili as a leader dapat kabalo ka or as a fiscal manager kabalo ka kung unsa ang imohang accountability did2 sa mga tao kay once mahimo nimo na dili na sila mangutana sa imoha but imo nan ang gipangita na anon a sila ang trust ba once you establish kaning trust no na nakuha nimo ang trust sa tao mao na imong authority as a fiscal manager ing.ana lang akoang medyo kuan.

- **JESON**

Same thing with them initiator and you should act as the leader rather than being a manager because leader knows hows to listen communicate with the members and also at the same time to follow kung what is right and must .be guided with the legal basis base on the answer of maam joana thank you.

b. being new with the job, how important it is for you to connect with the peers and mentors in the field to be able to gain more knowledge on this certain task?

- **JESON**

Very important because there is no such thing word, monopoly meaning monopoly of the knowledge and skills of leading people or handling a school so in my case personally I really love asking from my peer form my friends for a certain task on how to do it what we gonna do for me to submit a certain report as well as to handling a school is in focus.

- **LISARIE**

As a leader school leader kani struggle kaau nako ning mag connect kay personality nako kay dili ko ka ing.ana ka outgoing maa ba so siguro mao siguro kanong para sa akoa it's a call kay kabalo ko sa akoang kaugalingon nga dili ko ingon ana in which pag leader ka imoha gyud na syang himoon so importante kaau mag connect because there are a lot of things na sa imong huna huna sakto pero sa legally technically dili diay sya sakto. It is not enough na kannag in good faith ang imohang reason nga imo ning gihimo because not all people will understand that diba ikaw ray nakabalo nga ingon ana pero sa uban tao pag it will not serve them it will go against sa ilahang pagtuo because dili gyud na sya maau sa ilahang huna huna so ako lang I share kaning recent gyud sya kau .nga kanang panghutabo ba sa akong pagtan.aw gyud nako verygood na gyud kaau sya kaau naay nag ad2 sa amoa nga kanang amoang school farmers association and ingon niya they were recommended by the barangay captain na ang gulayan sa barangay ad2 ibutang as eskwelahan for that reason so ako at first niingon ko nga dili siguro sya mahimong kuan sa barangay it would be kaning under pa gyud gihapon sya sa gulayan sa paaralan but sige in partnership no sa akoang hunahuna it would be a good partnership sa akoang community ig sa swelahan nga did2 maghimo ug gulayan pero under sya sa GPP namo at the same time it could be the kaning laboratory man gud nga para sa amoang exploratory subject nga TLE nga agriculture nad maybe we can kaning inspire kning student na sa senior high school mukuha sila ug agriculture and we can kaning gain insights directly from farmers no ingon ana so lami na kaau akong hunahuna and then I ask somebody nga was it good is it a wise decision to accept kaning ingon.ani na proposal although gihatag sa akoa sa farmers asscociation sa barangay ang authority or ang tanan to propose something para masulod lang jud sya sa among skwelahan walay silay problema ana pero murag naa pa jud syay mga off and so nag kuan ko nag consult ko ug laing tao nga ana sya na what you did is wrong because unang una you are not the owner you are just a steward of the school you are of course the person in authority of the school but you are not the owner you are just a steward so kinsa man jud ang tag.iya sa skwelahan? Si kani so niingin sya so there for magpahibalo ka something ingon.ana no magpahibalo ka sa ilaha ingon ko it is in good faith nga ingon ani ilaha maning kuan program ang GPP niana sya nga baskin pa because it is not all about your program It is all about the kaning area nga ang mag teel ana is dili taga skwelahan ingon ko partnership man ingon sya maybe pwede artnership sya but have to put it into right thing you have this probem then you hae this mao ni mao na ay ingon ana so na off n apud ko na down na sad ko na kalami man unta sa akaong motibo and kuan and direction pero naa diay mga ingon ana even pa gyud diay kanang mga nag prutas sa imong school unya imohang ipapakyaw kuan ingon ko asa man ko mangutana ani? Ingon sya kay kinsa man ka nagdawat asa man gikan imo sweldo? Ingoon sya gikan sa cluster gikan sa division gikan sa region. Ingon ko nag ikan sa region then you have to write to the region ngano maam kay tungod kay sila ang mag clearance sa imo once mag retire ka ad all this naa ni sa imohang skwelahan pero muepekto ni karn wala pa ni per possible nga muapekto na sa imoha once naay mag file ug complain sa imoha youre retirement is as state. Hay na down n apud ko ka way lami aning mag school head oi

Pero maam wla nako ni sya na storya sa among mga kauban pud gyud sa deped like sila ni sir jeson sila ni maam jo wala nako ni sya gi stoya but this is kaning akong gipangay ang kuan ani gi consult nako sya fom a person outside deped private person na kabalo pud sya sa systema sa ingon ana lang pud so nakaingon ko Okay you have mao tung iyang ingon na ad2 did2 sa mao ni mao na ang you have to write letter you have to kuan your proposal and all then get their approval before you can go about that project mga ana maam so importante jud diay mag connect kay diri ka dili ka retire pag dili ka ka connect

- **JOANA**

Of course its very important jud jul no kay there are times also na although I like to solve problems pro naa juy time na pero dili man like wala pud jud koy choice kailanagan nako solbaron kung pwede wala nay problema but there are time times gyud na murag gihimo naman nako tanan nag huna huna na ko nganong dili dili nako sya masolbad so that's the time na kanang muad2 ko sa akong mentor nga mag naa pa gyud diay syay wisdom nga pag sa iyaha ko mag open up ay anaon ra diay na sya masolbad diay ang ing.ana then that's why that very important gyud especially kanang mga season nga bag.o pa man me no lahi ra pud gyud ang ang wisdom gyud sa season principals ug mentors.

YOU so your like saying now maam na they are seeing bigger picture than you are

Yes murag sa akoa lisod na peo sa ilaha sayon ra diay basic

- **LISARIE**

Once gyud diay pud ma na kanang other person gyud day. Naa gyud diay ni isa gyud diya sa timan an nato na once pag naa ta sa work kung naa ta within the box dili gyud nato maki-ta ang dako na problema so it really helps kung naa kay connection or naka connect kag lain tao kay because sila man gud gawas man gud sila sa box so makitan dayon nila ang all corners ng box and asa ka mag go wrong so dapat naa gyud ka makaconnect gyud kag mga peers and mentors.

c. how significant it is for you to be literate in fiscal management?

- **JOANA**

Very important gyud sya kay diba mao to akong ingon na ikaw man gyud gipahimo nimo sa uban pero pagmagkamali na ikaw man gihapon ang accountable so dpaat ikaw gyud mismo kabalo jud ka sa process and mao ng usahay mag handson gyud ko sa mga dapat buluha-ton sa school head although naa man gyuy time na edelegate nako n o pero katong mga basic na dapat gina trabaho sa school head dapat letirate ug kabalo gyud ta sa process para pud na sa amoa the for example karon naay mga monitoring makabalo me unsaon gani na ah mao diay na dili kay kanang manawag pami sa amoang teachers so unsa amon itubag so boomerang gihapon sa amoa so we need to be literate

YOU: so one of the your saying din maam no na one of the ways that showing that you are literate is your bale to do it yourself.

- **LISARIE**

Very significant kay mao gyud ni sya ang kasagaran reason kaning fiscal management pag ma wrong sya murag syag kasagaran reason ng mahimong immature ang imuhang retire-ment kay naa kay mga kaso ano gyud sya kaau planning siguro clerical work pwede siguro nimo say I delegate pero when it comes to planning monjtoring and evaluation dapat ikaw jud and dili ka makahimo ug isa ka sakto na monitoring kung wa ka kasabot no kung dili ka literate sa fiscal management so it would be ang planning nimo mo haom sa imohang evaluation kung naa kay skills sa monitoring and mao na sya ang isa sa mga reasons sa monitoring na kasabot gyud ka kay di jud ka ka monitor sa tinood lang muingon lang ka na nag monitor ka pero wla gyud ka ka monitor gyud kung unsay nahitabo kung wala ka kasabot sa kwarta unsay resources.

- **JESON**

Hoe significant no to be literate grabe jud ang question to be literate jud jul sige nalang oi. Anyway kuan sya very significant why because you are the head you are the hope of the entity you are the head of the procurement entity so if we will talk about fiscal management meaning accountability and transparency wise sa imoha man sya tanan so for me significant kaau say jul mao lang to thank you. Para mahuman na ta oi.

d. why do you think you need to be transparent as fiscal manager?

- **LISARIE**

Education because being ka school leader you have also the responsibility to educate you subordinates so kannag transparency it is not just showing kung asa niad2 ang kwarta but it is also educating them naalign ba ning atoang pang gasto sa atoang instruction? Ang gain ba ani niad2 sa learning improvement ng mga bata or learning outcome sa mga bata something like that because while dili na kau concern sa teacher ng kaning fiscal dira man gud nila makit.an na ah okay ang direction kay miski unsaon man gud nimo usahay naay times jud na maski unsaon nimo balikbalik ang direction sa imohang skwelahan kung asa mo padulong dili na kahinumdom si teacher ana not unless naa syay makit.an na ay everymonth naa diay ta transparency board makit.an na niya na ay ing.ani diay padung diay diria mao diay ni ilahang gina himo so atleast at the same time maka question sila during planning makita nila nan ga ah mao ni ang implementation karon ah sa kuan transparent ka did nila Nakita kung pila ang imohang gi alote ani na mag programs and all and masabtan nila kung I mean basta in other ways kung kuan na sya maam its educating the kaning the whole organization kung ang imohang ang plan ba nimo ah sakto ba ang implementation nimo sa imong mga activity basi sa inyohang plan.

- **JESON**

One work lang man ang form ni its VALUES ana jud si maam Lisarie education for me its values teaching them the right values because it will emanate them the idea of being honest na honest diay si kuan ana ang school head but aside form it no if we will follow the code of conduct a teacher and a profession it is we are in the position that we need to be open in the public we can read that one to kuan no the code of ethics naan a sya nakabutang a teacher and a profession na we are open from a public scrutiny meaning whatever the resources incurred in a specific school or by the school head it must be open to everybody for scrutiny and from that I mean kuan sya dira sya ma correct if unsa pa ang necessary na materials needed you can identify the pros and the cons or the dos and the donts so very sya essential if we will have the values system ang purpose nimo and aside from the following the code of ethics thank you.

- **JOANA**

  For them to experience share responsibility diba you need to be transparent to them for them also to know the process.

e. how essential it is to process positive and good attitude as a school leader particularly in handling school resources.?

- **LISARIE**

  very essential kay gi storya naman n ani sr jeson kaganina maam no na kanang banag you are kaning subject to public scrutiny murag ana ba once makapakita ka ug negative na attitude dira as grabe ang impact ng kaning school resources maam sa career sa mga school leader so very essential sya kay maguba ra gyud ka sa pila ka sentabo tanan ang imohang tibuok dignidad ug credibilidad maguba ng wa nabalik ug as ana diba.

- **JESON**

  Yes very essential the same thing with maam lisarie that we need to possess the positive and good attitude because aside from following the legal basis no as to resources scripture we are the best visual aid for in the eyes of many not only for the teacher not only for the students parents but ofcourse the entire community even by walking outside the school campus for pag uli pa nimo gina tan.aw naka and it would reflect also the way you lead your school that means possess positively handling resources and despite of all blends countered you should remain in humane you should remain in a nice manner padown lang gyud ka because in our work humility is the key dili jud pwede ang mapag mataas kay you should dili pud sya ma achive nimo ang kuan no maybe there are moments in your life nga da mas kuan pa ko yeah its true however at the end of the day you need to reflect on nan aa puy mga purpose or reason why it was happened ana gud sya so thank you and good afternoon.

- **JOANA**

  Of course its very essential no na positive jud ka naa kay good attitude or else masiradong skwelahan diba so ikaw mismo kanang taasan pa jud kung positive ka ka I positive pa gyud ana sya para makapadayon ang skwelahan you need to be a good steward no sa mga school resources stewardship.

  ONE SENTENCE NA PINAKA NA LEARN NINYO AS SCHOOL HEAD SO FAR.

- **LISARIE**

Set aside your personal motive when you work sa department of education because daghan kaau siguro sobra fifty percent ang naa dinha especially sa public school kana bitawng unlovable kaau na mga ano but as a teacher as a school leader you really have to kaning imoha ng I iigo I love na nimo tanan and the ang isa pa gyud na na learn nako is kaning accountability ug kanang ambot lang maam oi basta ako maam makahilak lang ko mag tan. aw sa kanan bitawng mag disappoint ko ma tan aw kanan bitawng hala oi wala man diay ni nako sila na storyahan ani no nya usahay pag makakita ko ug kanang teacher nako na kanang bitawng labad sa ulo ma blame nako akoang self nga kablo man gyud ko na labad ni sya no luoya niya no ingani lang diay kutob ang iyang panlantaw something ana ba and na ba and the disappointment muad2 sya sa ako ba nah ala wala na diay ko nahimo ani niya maong ingon ani ni sya so as of karon maam siguro mga one year pa man ko nga school head gyud no daghan pa kaau ang muabot no daghan pa kaau naka unsa an mga butang na kargahunon no kanang daghan pa kaau ko makat.unan pero basta ako lang gyud main-gon na kanang do kung kanang unsa ang makaayo para sa mga bata basta ang akoang motto kanang serve the least of your brethren murag ana maam ba na kung kinsa tung pinakaubos sa imong community mao toy I serve nimo not anybody sa imohang skwelahan. And you really have to put your loyalty sa imong studyante dili sa skwelahan dili sa imong school head not even sa imong supervisors put loyalty sa imong mga bata because you will never go wrong pag did2 ang imohang loyaty sa ilaha.

- **JOANA**

Leadership is not an easy and a glamourous job as what others think it involves sacrifice risk devotion and clarity of mind so every now and then you will experience na you will be critize even how good your intention and that's parts of leadership apil nana sya sa sweldo so together with praise you also need to embrace criticism with a strong heart leadership is indeed a gift from GOD and deffinetly not for the painted heart but now matter how difficult the journey will be GOD ssaid that my grace is sufficient for you be strong and courageous for I will be with you so if its your gift is leadership then lead.

- **JESON**

Before anything else Lesson that I have learn with my experiences as school head I would like to reflect that one and to intergrate that one to different part of our body so number one is brain. So as a school head no what thing ive learn is we need to use our brain especially in planning and moyivating people around as our teachers personal our teachers and the community the second one is out heart ive learned that not always that we should adhere to the legal basis that in toto we need to follow but of course we need we need also to feel what they feel so that is the heart. The third one is our ear I know how to listen people I know how to listen the problems and the challenges experienced by my teachers my parents and even my students. And the last one is my hand this is one way that I should act as a doer and not just a listener and not just a school head but I should serve as a role model for them to follow what I I have started so meaning brain the head the heart the ear and the hands and lastly sometimes we should be selective in our battle peace is better than being right.

PEER DEBRIEFING CERTIFICATE

PEER DEBRIEFING CERTIFICATE

This is to certify that the study entitled "Travalls of Novice Principals as Fiscal Managers" has been validated by the undersigned.

As observed, the researcher has employed a rich source of data to establish credibility. Further, the researcher provided a comprehensive discussion allowing other researchers to make reasonable judgment about the transferability of the result in a different setting.

Signature: _____

Name: CORAZON G. CABALLES

Position: School Principal 2

Institution: DepEd-Communal ES

MEMBER CHECK CERTIFICATE

University of Mindanao
Professional Schools

MEMBER CHECK CERTIFICATE

After carefully reading and checking the transcription of the in-depth interview held last March 6, 2022 regarding the travails of the novice principals as fiscal managers, conducted by the researcher herself, JULIE ANN D. BAYANI, I hereby attest to the truthfulness and accuracy of the data. I therefore categorically declare it as the same information that I have provided during the interview, and that those words were same words I uttered in response to the researcher's queries.

I have likewise checked the summarized transition that the investigator has kindly provided and found them to be exact representation of my account on the travails of novice principals as fiscal managers.

Among other things, the researcher has also correctly described the circumstances surrounding the said interview namely the time and place of the meeting and has kept the word, that she will provide me the opportunity to verify the information I have given during the interview.

PARTICIPANT: _____

Signature: _____

Date: _____ March 30, 2022 _____

University of Mindanao
Professional Schools

MEMBER CHECK CERTIFICATE

After carefully reading and checking the transcription of the in-depth interview held last March 6, 2022 regarding the travails of the novice principals as fiscal managers, conducted by the researcher herself, JULIE ANN D. BAYANI, I hereby attest to the truthfulness and accuracy of the data. I therefore categorically declare it as the same information that I have provided during the interview, and that those words were same words I uttered in response to the researcher's queries.

I have likewise checked the summarized transition that the investigator has kindly provided and found them to be exact representation of my account on the travails of novice principals as fiscal managers.

Among other things, the researcher has also correctly described the circumstances surrounding the said interview namely the time and place of the meeting and has kept the word, that she will provide me the opportunity to verify the information I have given during the interview.

PARTICIPANT: ███████████████

Signature: ███████████████

Date: _____ March 30, 2022 _____

University of Mindanao
Professional Schools

MEMBER CHECK CERTIFICATE

After carefully reading and checking the transcription of the in-depth interview held last March 6, 2022 regarding the travails of the novice principals as fiscal managers, conducted by the researcher herself, JULIE ANN D. BAYANI, I hereby attest to the truthfulness and accuracy of the data. I therefore categorically declare it as the same information that I have provided during the interview, and that those words were same words I uttered in response to the researcher's queries.

I have likewise checked the summarized transition that the investigator has kindly provided and found them to be exact representation of my account on the travails of novice principals as fiscal managers.

Among other things, the researcher has also correctly described the circumstances surrounding the said interview namely the time and place of the meeting and has kept the word, that she will provide me the opportunity to verify the information I have given during the interview.

PARTICIPANT: _____

Signature: _____

Date: _____March 30, 2022_____

MEMBER CHECK CERTIFICATE

After carefully reading and checking the transcription of the in-depth interview held last March 6, 2022 regarding the travails of the novice principals as fiscal managers, conducted by the researcher herself, JULIE ANN D. BAYANI, I hereby attest to the truthfulness and accuracy of the data. I therefore categorically declare it as the same information that I have provided during the interview, and that those words were same words I uttered in response to the researcher's queries.

I have likewise checked the summarized transition that the investigator has kindly provided and found them to be exact representation of my account on the travails of novice principals as fiscal managers.

Among other things, the researcher has also correctly described the circumstances surrounding the said interview namely the time and place of the meeting and has kept the word, that she will provide me the opportunity to verify the information I have given during the interview.

PARTICIPANT: _____

Signature: _____

Date: _____ March 30, 2022 _____

University of Mindanao
Professional Schools

MEMBER CHECK CERTIFICATE

After carefully reading and checking the transcription of the in-depth interview held last March 6, 2022 regarding the travails of the novice principals as fiscal managers, conducted by the researcher herself, JULIE ANN D. BAYANI, I hereby attest to the truthfulness and accuracy of the data. I therefore categorically declare it as the same information that I have provided during the interview, and that those words were same words I uttered in response to the researcher's queries.

I have likewise checked the summarized transition that the investigator has kindly provided and found them to be exact representation of my account on the travails of novice principals as fiscal managers.

Among other things, the researcher has also correctly described the circumstances surrounding the said interview namely the time and place of the meeting and has kept the word, that she will provide me the opportunity to verify the information I have given during the interview.

PARTICIPANT: _____

Signature: _____

Date: _____ March 30, 2022 _____

University of Mindanao
Professional Schools

MEMBER CHECK CERTIFICATE

After carefully reading and checking the transcription of the in-depth interview held last March 6, 2022 regarding the travails of the novice principals as fiscal managers, conducted by the researcher herself, JULIE ANN D. BAYANI, I hereby attest to the truthfulness and accuracy of the data. I therefore categorically declare it as the same information that I have provided during the interview, and that those words were same words I uttered in response to the researcher's queries.

I have likewise checked the summarized transition that the investigator has kindly provided and found them to be exact representation of my account on the travails of novice principals as fiscal managers.

Among other things, the researcher has also correctly described the circumstances surrounding the said interview namely the time and place of the meeting and has kept the word, that she will provide me the opportunity to verify the information I have given during the interview.

PARTICIPANT: _____

Signature: _____

Date: _____ March 30, 2022 _____

NVIVO

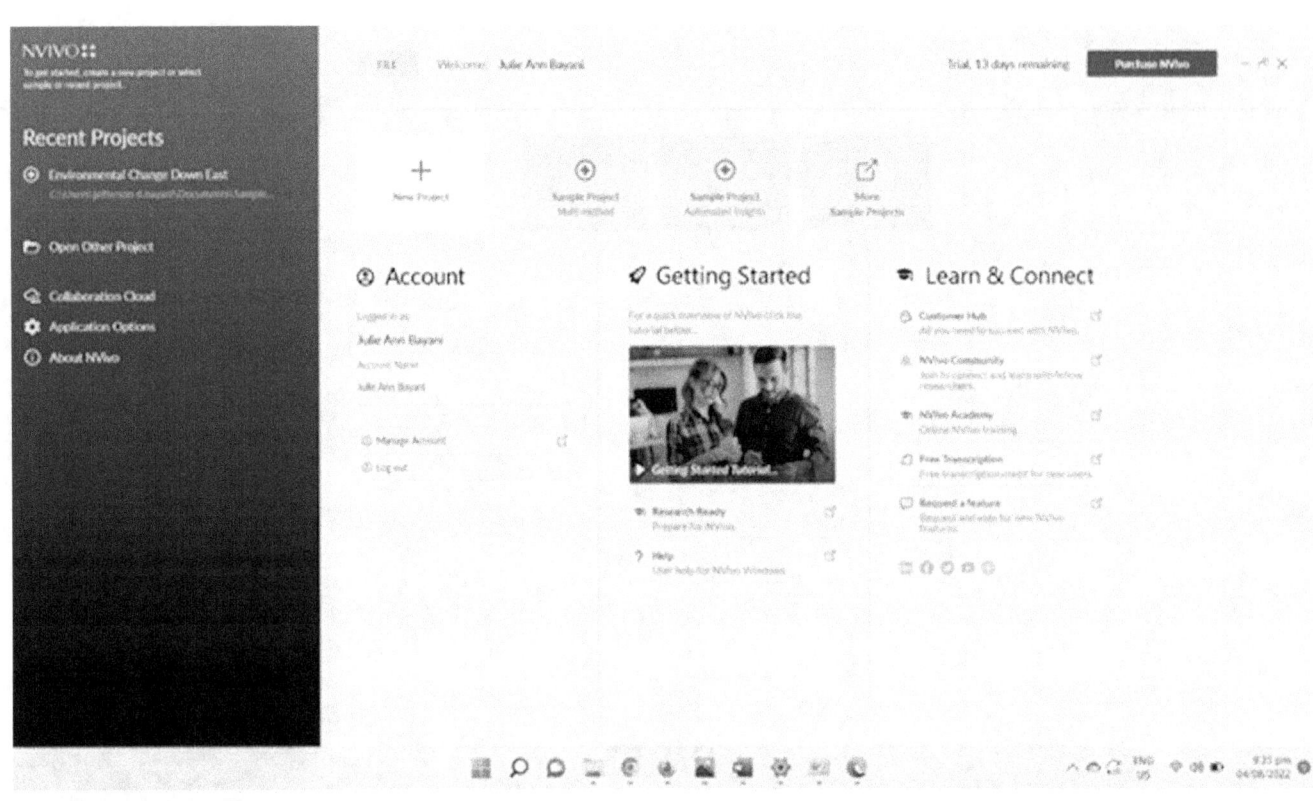

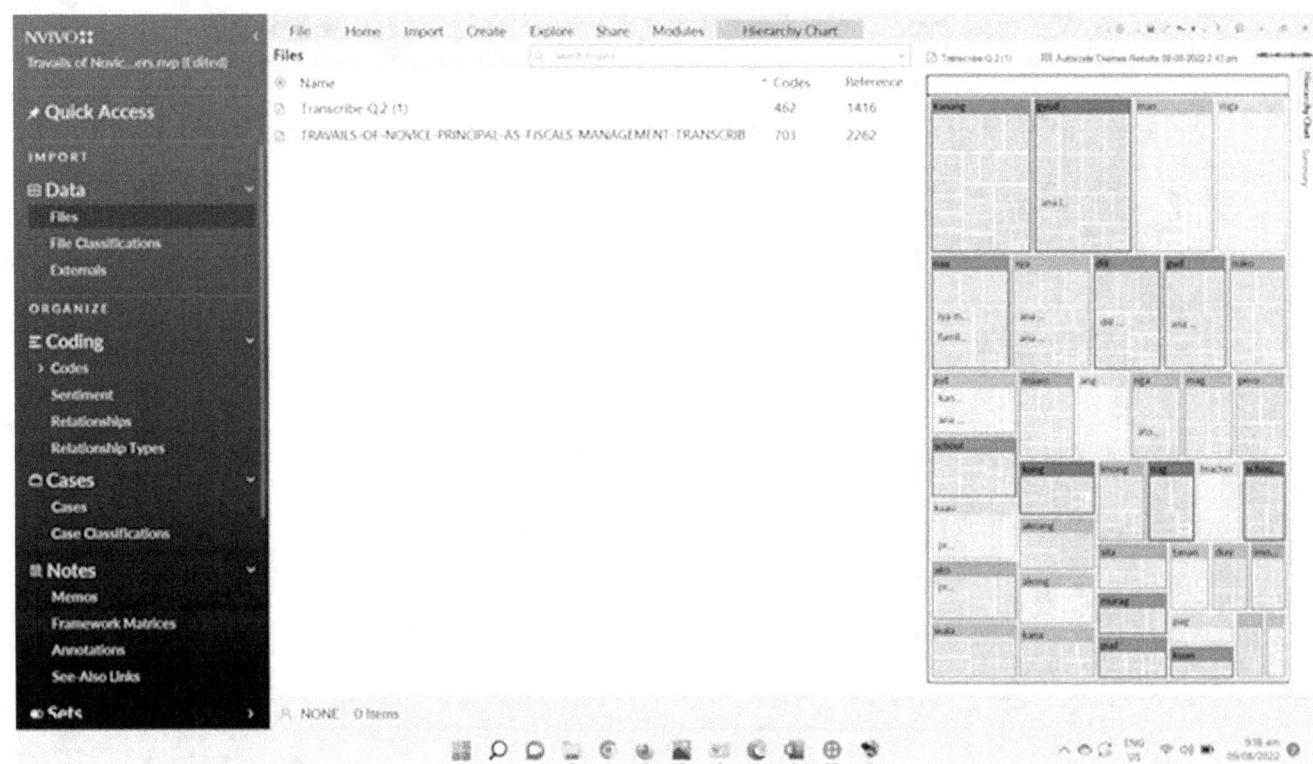

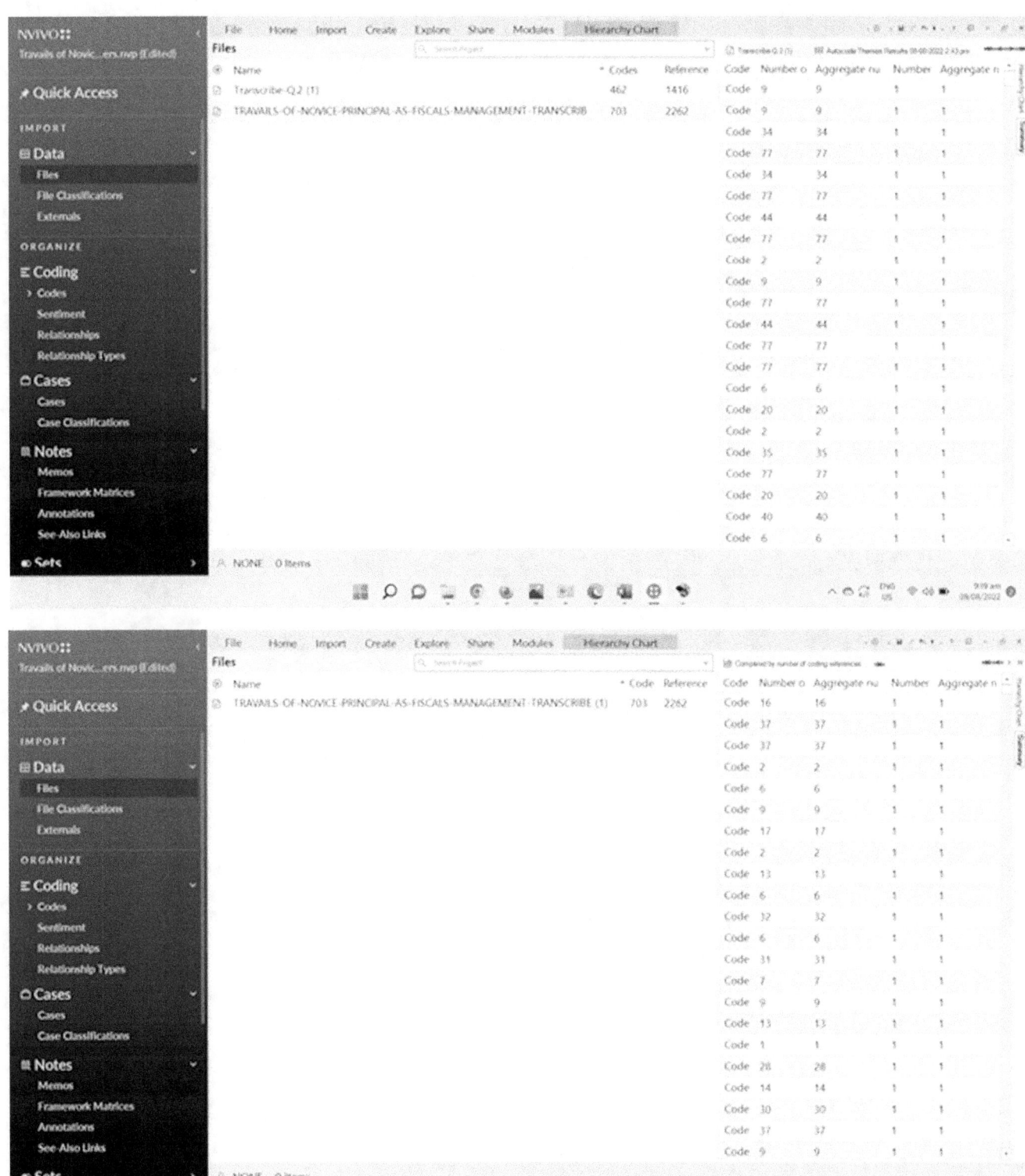

PLAGIARISM CHECK RECEIPT

Digital Receipt

This receipt acknowledges that Turnitin received your paper. Below you will find the receipt information regarding your submission.

The first page of your submissions is displayed below.

Submission author:	Julie Ann Bayani
Assignment title:	PS 2019-2020
Submission title:	TRAVAILS OF NOVICE PRINCIPALS AS FISCAL MANAGERS
File name:	FINAL_MANUSCRIPT_BAYANI_1.docx
File size:	5.33M
Page count:	140
Word count:	32,385
Character count:	160,301
Submission date:	18-Jan-2023 03:45PM (UTC+0800)
Submission ID:	1994654908

TRAVAILS OF NOVICE PRINCIPALS AS FISCAL MANAGERS

JULIE ANN B. BAYANI

GRAMMARLY CHECK CERTIFICATE

The University of Mindanao

CERTIFICATION

To Whom It May Concern:

This is to certify that the manuscript of **Ms. Julie Ann D. Bayani,** entitled **"Travails of Novice Principals as Fiscal Managers",** has been checked and edited by the undersigned.

This certification is issued on January 29, 2023.

ANA HELENA R. LOVITOS, PhD, MedStud

Reader

CURRICULUM VITAE

CURRICULUM VITAE

JULIE ANN D. BAYANI

Block 75, Lot 5, Deca Homes, Tigatto, Davao City

Mobile Number: 09514551847

Email-address: bayanijulieann11@gmail.com

Orcid id: 0000-0002-0160-1807

PERSONAL INFORMATION

Nickname: Ann

Birthday: July 11, 1991

Birthplace: Davao City

Age: 31

Nationality: Filipino

Religion: Christian

Civil Status: Single

Father's Name: Joselito A. Bayani

Mother's Name: Dahlia D. Bayani

EDUCATIONAL BACKGROUND

Tertiary: University of Southeastern Philippines

Secondary: Davao City National High School

Elementary: Sta. Ana Central Elementary School

EMPLOYMENT BACKGROUND

2017 – Present: Communal National High School, DepEd

2013 – 2016: Tumble Tots Philippines